Bags

A LEXICON OF STYLE

Bags

A Lexicon Of Style

Written by Valerie Steele
& Laird Borrelli

SCRIPTUM EDITIONS
LONDON · HONG KONG

Publisher *Beatrice Vincenzini*

Executive Director *David Shannon*

Editorial Director *Alexandra Black*

Art Director *David Mackintosh*

Project Coordinator *Charlotte Wilton-Steer*

Picture Researcher *Laird Borrelli*

Studio Photography *Fred Corcoran*

Illustrator *Tanya Ling*

First published in the UK by Scriptum Editions

Created by Co & Bear Productions (UK) Ltd.

Printed and bound in Novara, Italy by Officine Grafiche de Agostini.

First edition

10 9 8 7 6 5 4 3 2 1

ISBN 1-902686-04-7

Photograph on previous page: Regan Cameron for Francesco Biasia.

Illustration this page: Tanya Ling.

Overleaf: illustration of denim Fendi Baguettes by Hiroshi Tanabe.

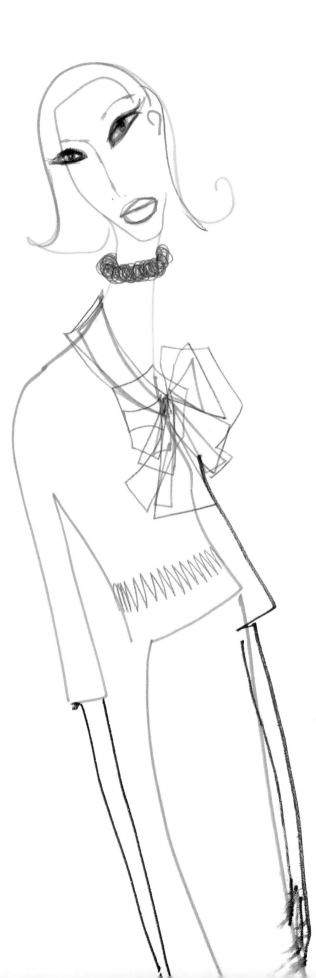

CONTENTS

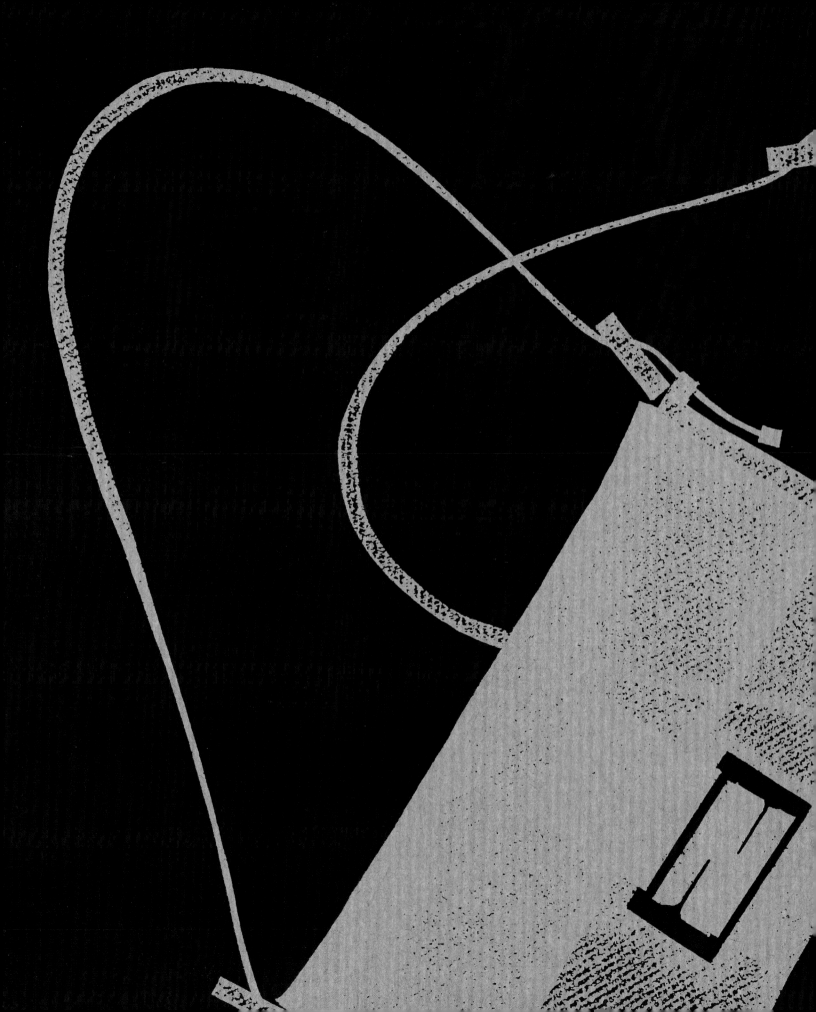

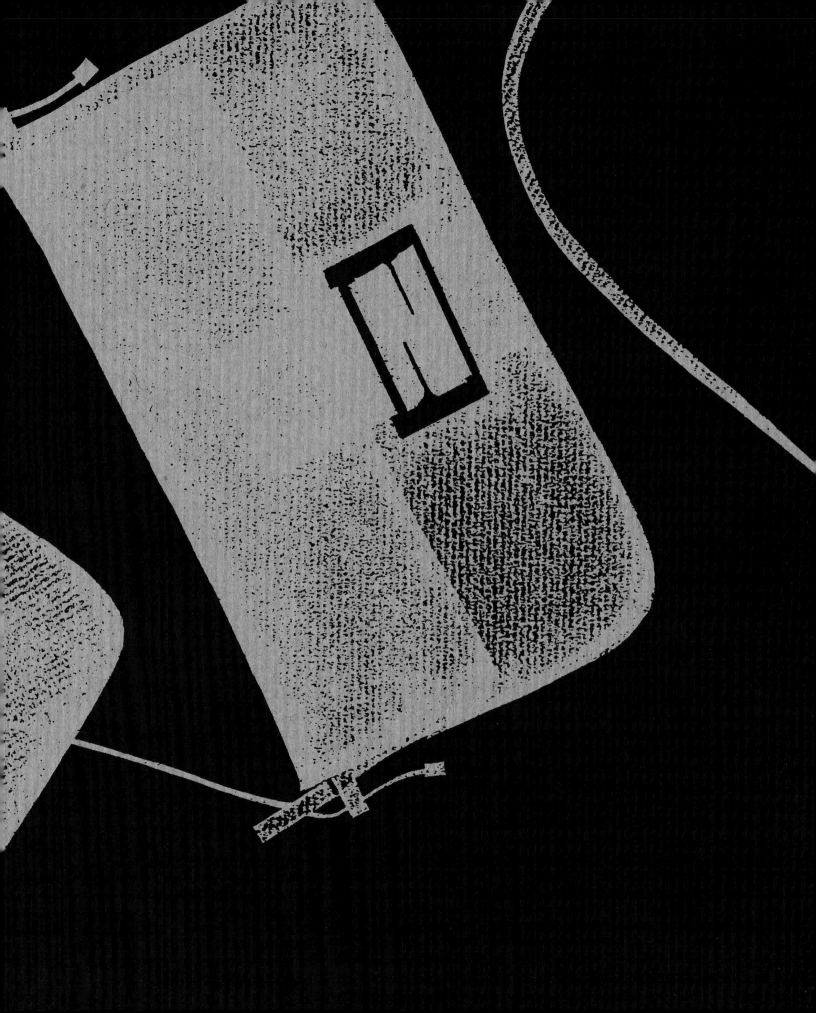

introduction

"Ever since handbags have become part of fashion they have helped to define our individuality and identity."[1]

Claire Wilcox

Bags are hot. "Handbag mania" dominates fashion. As *Vogue*'s Mimi Spencer observes, if you consider the leading fashion companies of today, "what hits you like a brick is that it's bags, not clothes, that are the key to their success."[2]

Why are bags so popular today? If we analyze handbag mania in terms of fashion trends, the answer can be summed up in the word "money." There is money to be made in bags, especially those regarded as status symbols. In addition, as clothing fashions have become increasingly minimal, accessories such as bags and shoes have taken on correspondingly greater importance. If we look at the broader social picture, it is also clear that bags play a significant role in women's changing lives. Women tend to carry a lot around with them, because their bags serve so many practical purposes – as an office away from the desk, a portable dressing table, a survival kit. But bags are not purely functional, either. On the individual level, the bag is a psychologically and aesthetically significant object, an artwork in which we "carry our neuroses."[3]

This book explores the social, sartorial, and psychological significance of bags. It is not a history of bags, although it does place today's fashions within an historical context. The first chapter is devoted to Practical bags. Among the questions posed are fundamental ones, such as: Why do women carry bags? How can men function without bags? What do women carry in their bags? Modern women have increasingly assumed new roles, while also retaining many of their traditional aspirations. As a result, they use different kinds of bags for a variety of different purposes. In the nineteenth century, the fashionable woman carried a tiny purse containing her visiting cards, a small amount

ABOVE Women use bags for a variety of different purposes and often carry more than one bag. It is not unusual for a woman to store a smaller, daintier bag within a larger tote, as this Desmo model has done. *Esquire* magazine describes the former as a "dinghy" and the latter as "the mother ship."

of money, and a handkerchief. No "nice" woman wore cosmetics or worked at an office. By the mid-twentieth century, the average woman needed a larger bag, because she was away from home working, shopping, and socializing.

Yet practical bags, such as satchels and totes, are only part of the picture. The second chapter, Precious, focuses on pretty little bags – usually evening bags – that barely have room for keys, make-up, and money. They are certainly not practical, but they make a visual statement. Like jewelry, they tend to be characterized by precious materials, artistic workmanship, and feminine iconography. Both decorative and personal, precious bags provide an element of fantasy and charm that is not always evident in more functional day bags.

The third chapter deals with Status bags, the "die-for-it" bags with labels and logos that translate into big money and instant prestige. Like a successful fragrance, an important trend bag is central to the image (and finances) of major fashion concerns. Women who want the status associated with designer fashion – without buying into the entire look – often just take the bag.

In the 1980s fashionable women overwhelmingly took the classic Chanel bag, but a decade later there were many more choices. In 1997, for example, Christian Dior sold approximately 140,000 of that year's hot bag, the Lady Dior. Each one cost around $1,200. Tom Ford of Gucci has thought a lot about what makes a particular bag hot. He emphasizes the importance of good design and craftsmanship, while also acknowledging that a recognized name is also an asset. Celebrity clients and editorial coverage help, too. "If all that is pleasing, it will sell. More than that, it's like you gotta have it or you'll die."[4]

Whereas the significance of the status bag centers on its name or logo – all those Gs, Cs and LVs – there is another, related type of bag that is the focus of the fourth chapter. Luxury bags are primarily distinguished by the quality of their materials and craftsmanship, and by the beauty of their design. It may no longer be chic to be a label snob, but many women are still attracted to sumptuous, expensive bags or those that aspire to the status of artworks.

Luxury also implies voluptuous pleasure, and as Charlotte Skene-Catling writes in her introduction to Nathalie Hambro's book, *The Art of the Handbag*: "All good design, and particularly fashion with its obvious relation to the body, becomes a fetishistic process; one of imbuing inanimate objects with a magical or spiritual quality. The covert pleasure of sliding a hand into a hidden interior has obvious potential for an urban fetishist …"[5] Bags are not only functional survival kits, precious objects, and expensive status symbols, they are also intensely personal receptacles.

The fifth and final chapter, Utility, deals with the most current trend. Whereas the chic woman has traditionally held her bag in her hand or slung it over her shoulder, today she simply straps it on her body. The new utility bags are buckled around the waist, strapped on the hip, or worn on the back. Indeed, the popularity of the backpack is comparable to that of denim jeans, which also began as functional workwear and became a revolutionary fashion icon for both men and women. Inspired by military equipment and sportsgear, utility bags are *the* accessories for today's urban nomads. The bag has not only become an extension of our clothing; it is, literally, an extension of ourselves.

ABOVE LEFT & BELOW Utility bags, such as Matt Murphy's backpack which is engineered to sit flat against the back, are considered by some to be the perfect millennial accessory. Others will continue to be attached to status bags like Versace's bright red tote – because they feel the logo marks them apart from the crowd.

chapter one Practical

practical

"For many women the tote bag is an office away from the desk, a portable dressing table, a locker room, lunch-pail, library, shopping cart, travel bag, or an amalgam of all of these."[1]

Carrie Donovan

ABOVE Practical bags with soft constructions, like this one by Nannini, can morph to accommodate various contents. **OPPOSITE** Max Mara reinterprets the classic bucket bag in bright yellow leather. The shoulder straps leave the hands free and the wearer ready for action. Photograph by Steven Meisel.

"Men don't need purses. Men manage to walk around with the three essentials (comb, wallet, keys) tucked neatly into their pockets."[2] Women, on the other hand, seem to carry everything but the kitchen sink. Obviously, this sexual division of labor is not absolute: Men do, after all, carry briefcases and gym bags. A few men even carry – or wear – unisex utility bags. Nevertheless, it must be admitted that men do not habitually carry as much stuff around with them as women tend to.

Letty Cottin Pogrebin once ruefully noted that women, "in Simone de Beauvoir's words, 'the second sex' – are also 'the schlepper sex.'"[3] As a traditional feminist, Pogrebin blamed society for forcing women to pay more attention to fashion than function. She also pointed out that women's clothes "have skimpy pockets," whereas men's clothes have "copious pockets for a wallet, glasses, keys or whatever."[4] There may be an element of truth to this, and yet even the most copious pockets would not hold everything that the average woman carries in her bag on a day-to-day basis.

Why do women carry so much in their bags? Why do they carry bags at all? History shows that in the past, before purses, women did carry things in their pockets. Bags first came into fashion in about 1800 when the full skirts of the *ancien régime* gave way to the slender, diaphanous dresses of the First Empire. Prior to that time, bags had been rather uncommon, since most women carried small necessities in the pockets hidden inside their full skirts. (The pockets were attached to a waistband, and were reached through slashes in the sides of the skirt.) It was only when the narrow, gauzy Neoclassical style of dress

OPPOSITE Construction, precision engineering, and functionalism
define practical bags. This streamlined tote by Swiss leathergoods
maker Bally exhibits all of these qualities.

eliminated the space for pockets that bags came into vogue. These early bags were known in England as "indispensibles," because they contained crucial impedimenta such as fans and visiting cards.

From the end of the eighteenth century to the early part of the twentieth, in both England and France, bags, made of string mesh, were commonly known as "reticules" or "reticles," a reference to their netted construction. In France a pun on the word reticule apparently led to purses sometimes being referred to as "ridicules," perhaps because it seemed amusing to see ladies carrying little bags that resembled previously hidden pockets. (In that respect, these bags evoke the modern phenomenon of underwear as outerwear.)

Once made, the transition from pocket to purse proved irreversible. There are, of course, utility bags for daytime that are worn on a waistband, as pockets used to be, but these are less common than handbags or shoulder bags. Fashion historian Claire Wilcox points out that changes in the role of women in society have affected the size, design, and function of bags. Over the course of the twentieth century, the basic bag has grown from a tiny drawstring purse to a substantial tote.

The fashionable lady of 1900 carried only a little reticule, containing visiting cards, a handkerchief, and a change purse. Anything larger was carried by a man – either the woman's husband or a porter. Only working-class women had to carry large packages themselves. A lady did not even have to carry house keys, because a servant would always be at home to let her in. Since cosmetics were still regarded as vaguely immoral, the lady carried only a discreet powder

ABOVE Some practical bags are utilitarian in their origins. The
bucket bag was directly inspired by its namesake. Bucket bags, like
this one by Rodo, remain a popular and practical style.

LEFT & OPPOSITE Straps keep the hands free. Nannini's sleek white envelope is engineered to sit neatly under the arm. Shiny metal hardware adds visual interest to the red bag by Perry Ellis.

BELOW Although most practical bags are made in leather, other kinds of materials can change the character of the bag. For example, Rodo's practical clutch in a hard techno material resembles a hand-held electronic gadget.

puff and a tiny bottle for perfume or smelling salts. It was not even necessary to carry much money, since most shopping was still charged to a family's account and delivered to the home.

As women's lives changed at the turn of the century so did their bags. Middle-class women began to spend more time outside the home, although few as yet were employed full-time. In 1900 the American mail order company Sears, Roebuck featured numerous handbags in their catalogue, ranging from chateleines to shopping bags. The chateleine was a little bag worn at the waist to carry money, keys, and small tools, such as scissors, which were used for home sewing. Waistbags had been worn as early as the Middle Ages by both men and women, but the late-nineteenth-century revival of the chateleine emphasized the medieval idea of the mistress of the house.

The housewife was not always at home, however. Shopping became a popular leisure activity as the retail revolution of the nineteenth century brought more and more products into the new department stores. Although stores still delivered many purchases, shopping bags began to be more widely used. Women also traveled for pleasure, and sets of luggage increasingly included small leather handbags designed to be kept with the traveler at all times. As women used handbags and carried money more often, pickpockets increasingly preyed on them. Handbag manufacturers had to develop safety catches and locking systems.

In the early twentieth century, more women began to engage in paid employment. Like their male counterparts, they now carried keys, wallets,

coin purses, and checkbooks, as well as handkerchiefs and combs. Furthermore, cosmetics ceased to be taboo, and by the 1920s began to be used extensively. Not only were cosmetics habitually carried about, they were also applied in public, although conservatives still frowned at the sight of women at restaurant tables reapplying their powder and lipstick.

As cosmetics became more popular, handbag makers incorporated mirrors and cosmetic cases. Fashion journalists advised women that it was "important to consider the interior of your bag. Do you load your bag with a lot of junk, or do you carry only a few well-chosen bag accessories? ... Of course, you will want a vanity, and if you can find one which includes the rouge and lipstick gadgets, it is far better than if they are placed separately in your bag."[5]

By the 1930s, most of the kinds of bags used today had already been invented, including the classic handbag with a clasp frame and handles, the clutch, the satchel, and even the shoulder bag. "Shoulder bags liberated the hands [and] were capacious enough for the practical needs of the working woman," writes Wilcox.[6] Elsa Schiaparelli was one of the first fashion designers to create shoulder bags, in the late 1930s. But the style really caught on during World War II, when practicalities were no longer a matter of choice. Paris was occupied by the Nazis, who commandeered all motorized vehicles for themselves. French women had to bicycle around the city and the shoulder bag provided obvious practical benefits. The style was also widely adopted in Great Britain and North America, as women increasingly entered the work force as part of the war effort.

ABOVE On a practical level, safety catches and locking systems are features added to practical bags and luggage in an attempt to repel pickpockets and thieves. On a purely visual level, they reinforce the notion that some of life's most valuable possessions are carried around in our bags.

LEFT Moschino-Redwall's perforated, see-through tote, photographed by Steve Hiett for *Vogue Italia*, displays the various and eccentric contents that practical bags can accommodate – including jellybeans. For the exhibitionist, a see-through bag provides a perfect medium for revelation, but many women shy away from sporting transparent bags, perhaps reluctant to put their intimate world on show.

ABOVE Totes are sometimes referred to as shoppers. These calf skin shoppers in animal prints by American design duo Lambertson Truex are perfect for coping in the urban jungle. The bag on the left has a soft construction, while the other is a structured tote, which has a more tailored look.

After the war ended, many women went back to the home, and roomy shoulder bags tended to be replaced by somewhat smaller handbags, as women no longer needed to carry around so much. These more petite styles were also in keeping with the lady-like look that was increasingly emphasized in the fashion press. Yet women continued to regard the bag as an important accessory.

Much of the fashion advice about bags recalled themes that had been well established by the 1930s. There was a strong emphasis on the rules of appropriate dress. "With a suit or a wool dress, the leather or tweed handbag, fitted with convenient toilet requirements, will sound just the right note," declared a book with the misleading title *Individuality and Clothes*. "The handbag may be chosen to harmonize with the costume in color, or it may be the color of the hat, shoes, and gloves."[7]

RIGHT & BELOW RIGHT Long, tall bags are called North-South or portrait bags, as opposed to East-West or landscape bags. Like Next's black leather tote, they often serve as an adjunct to a smaller bag such as this neat white one by Salvatore Ferragamo.

"Always the simplest and most classic handbags are the best and the quality of the leather is very important," advised Christian Dior's *Little Dictionary of Fashion*. Different bags were appropriate for day and evening, so it was necessary to have a minimum of two bags. "You can wear the same suit from morning to dinner – but to be really perfectly dressed you can not keep the same bag. For the morning it must be very simple and for the evening it must be smaller and, if you wish, a little more fancy." A good daytime style might be a black suede handbag, while for evening a gold kid clutch was suggested. The author (almost certainly not Dior himself) concluded sharply: "Don't forget, a bag is not a wastepaper basket! You can't fill it with a lot of unnecessary things and expect it to look nice and last a long time."[8]

Other arbiters of fashion insisted that the well-dressed woman needed a minimum of four handbags, all of good quality, "and quality, alas, is very often synonymous with expensive!" The essential four bags were:

1. *"A large bag for travel and casual wear. The height of luxury would be an alligator bag signed 'Hermès', but equally chic are the brass-trimmed Italian sports designs, as well as the American creations inspired by them.*

2. *An afternoon bag to wear with city ensembles and slightly dressy outfits. The most practical choice is undoubtedly a medium-sized bag of fine black calfskin with an attractive clasp. Suede is much more fragile and patent leather is never really elegant ...*

ABOVE Orion's tote, photographed by Stefano Paolillo, is made of leather and plastic. It is still considered taboo to look into another person's bag, yet many designers play with the idea of exposure by using translucent materials that reveal the contents of a bag.

RIGHT The Chloé girl can relax knowing that she's got style in spades, and lots of room to stow her things in her soft, roomy leather tote. It is big enough to contain everything she may need, even for an unexpected overnight stay.

OPPOSITE Old rules of appropriate dress required that shoes and bags coordinate with each other, and with one's outfit. Although times have changed, Missoni makes the matched look chic again as photographed by Mario Testino.

BELOW Etiquette deemed alligator a material that was strictly for daywear. Although the real thing is rarely used nowadays, it is often simulated in practical day bags, such as this one by Mulberry.

3. An evening purse of silk, satin, or velvet ...

4. For the summer, a beige straw bag ..."[9]

Under no circumstances should a woman "carry an alligator handbag with a dressy ensemble merely because she has paid an enormous sum of money for it. Alligator is strictly for sports and travel ... and this respected reptile should be permitted to retire every evening at 5 p.m."[10]

The rules governing "appropriate" dress relaxed considerably after the cultural upheavals of the 1960s led to an irreversible decline in formality. In addition, as more women began to have careers, they focused more on issues of practicality. Less practical bags were designed for pleasure – not to conform with the rules of propriety.

Since the nineteenth century the term handbag has referred to a functional leather bag. Traditionally, these bags were not made by dressmakers (who were predominantly female), but by leather workers (who were almost exclusively male). The majority of practical bags are still made from leather – in all its myriad manifestations, from dyed, embossed hide to suede. (Increasingly, however, bags are also made of "techno" fabrics, such as neoprene, which are light and weatherproof.) Many practical bags are essentially masculine and utilitarian in their origins. The bucket and the feed bags, for example, were directly inspired by their namesakes. Construction, engineering, and functionalism, rather than ornamentation, are prevalent characteristics of practical bags.

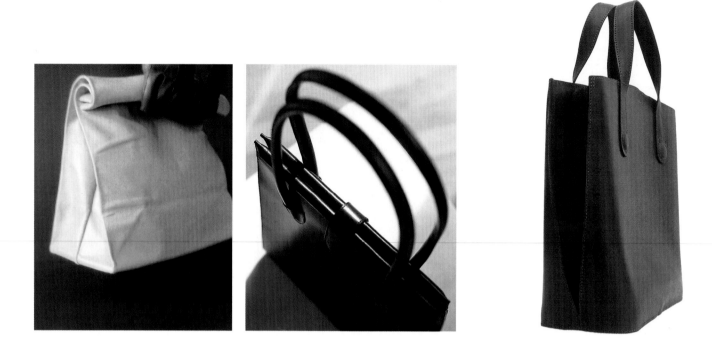

ABOVE LEFT A brown paper lunch bag inspired this bag, photographed by José van Riele. Practical bags are used to carry the impedimenta of quotidian life, from comestibles to hosiery. One informal study found that the average woman carries about forty-seven items in her bag.

ABOVE CENTER & RIGHT Bill Amberg is a master at engineering functional bags, whether slim, sleek, and shoulder friendly, or with a gusset to increase the bag's capacity.

Ruffo, for example, designs a line of accessories called "Origami Express," because of their versatility; you can expand them and fold them up. Designer Matt Murphy, whose engineered bags he describes as "tools," created a bag in which file folders could neatly hang.

The most basic practical bag is the tote bag, sometimes called a "shopper." The tote is adapted from the basic paper shopping bag and is top handled. Charlotte McKeough's "Brave Brown Bag" line of bags, made of weatherproof cotton twill, is inspired by the paper shopping bag. In fact, the paper shopping bag is an important category of bags in and of itself. Every shopper recognizes classic examples, such as Bloomingdale's big brown bag, Lord & Taylor's white paper bag with its distinctive rose, or Harrod's green and gold bag. East-West style totes (bags which are wider than they are high, as opposed to tall, narrow North-South styles) include the classic L.L. Bean canvas boat tote, Hervé Chapelier's colorful nylon zipped tote, and the carpetbag.

The satchel is a hand-held bag that comes in many variations, but always with a flat bottom and a top closing. It usually has two handles or straps and

BELOW RIGHT Tod's Hippy bag is an exquisitely crafted suede pouch of eight flat pieces puzzled together. It can be worn bandoleer style across the body in the same way as a military bag.

is often designed as a "convertible," meaning that the handles or straps can be adjusted or removed. Roberta di Camerino's Bagonghi bag is based on a doctor's satchel. Bucket, drawstring, and feed bag styles are round-bottomed shoulder bags. Bucket bags were particularly popular in the fifties, as these open-topped bags required less material. This was important in the postwar period, since there were shortages of many materials. The bucket bag was thus exempt from purchase tax.

The duffle bag, inspired by soldiers' kit bags, is a kind of zippered, sideways bucket bag. Other common shoulder bag styles include the Hobo and the school or messenger bag. The Hobo is a soft bag that bends in the middle when hung from the shoulder, whereas the school/messenger/bike bag is wide, and often gusseted with a top flap. Examples of this type of bag include Bottega Veneta's upgrade of the school bag, rendered in white woven leather, and Manhattan Portage bags which have been co-opted from bicycle messengers by the style-conscious. Practical bags, in their many different shapes and styles, "are the bags at the vanguard of style ... [with] the wherewithal to work magic with your wardrobe."[11]

Practical bags are at the vanguard of style because they are the bags most crucial to women on a daily basis. Common to all these bags are their functional origins – they are designed to carry the necessities of everyday life.

So why do women carry so much in their bags? Maverick feminist Germaine Greer suggests that bags link women to archaic roles: "Shouldering luggage is

BELOW Bottega Veneta is famous for its woven leather accessories, seen here close-up. Skilled leather workers make functional leather bags like these. In contrast, precious bags, which are often made of fabric, are sometimes referred to as dressmaker's bags, implying that they were made by women.

OPPOSITE This woven bag by Bottega Veneta is made of a semi-transparent hi-tech material. Designers are increasingly using techno materials to create clothing and accessories. These new materials express modernity, and are influencing the direction of contemporary fashion.

OPPOSITE Could Eva have possibly left something out of her capacious cK Calvin Klein tote? Practical bags this big can serve as virtual offices or dressing rooms.

an ancient female habit, born of servitude."[12] In reality, though, women seem to have begun carrying more, the more they have assumed hitherto male roles – while still carrying out traditional female roles, including that of the caretaker.

In his article, "The Content of Women's Purses: An Accessory in Crisis," sociologist Daniel Harris argues that when more women began working and new opportunities opened to them, their purses began to get bigger and fuller. "It was as if, in exchanging [roles], women created on their own person a microcosm of 'home,' a cache of talismanic articles suggestive of the domestic world's intimacy and security." The purse and its contents, according to Harris, preserve "the three abandoned personae that a woman has largely forgotten – the survivalist, the curator, and the homemaker."[13] There is something to be said for this thesis, although it is overstated.

ABOVE Hervé Chapelier's mini-shoppers are much sought after and come in a huge array of cool color combinations. This zip-top tote is made of nylon, which has the advantage of being both lightweight and weatherproof. Nylon also requires much less care than leather.

The persona of the survivalist is clearly significant, since, as Harris observes, many women "boast of the readiness with which they could face unforeseen disasters."[14] Journalist Betsy Israel, for example, says that "With a well-stocked purse, we are theoretically set for anything."[15] In *The New York Times*, Enid Nemy quotes a friend as saying "I could spend the night on the subway, if necessary. My handbag is a life-support system." Ultimately, Nemy concludes that "what a woman considers essential is on a different scale, a far grander and more imaginative level than men could ever dream of."[16]

According to the *Esquire* article "Your Wife: An Owner's Manual. Her Handbag: Its Capacity and Contents": "In movies, ideal ladies had tiny purses with tiny things in them." In "real life," however, "the purse of a married

ABOVE The briefcase is now a unisex practical bag, where once it belonged wholly in the male domain. This slim, tan version is by luxury goods maker Celine.

BELOW Dooney & Bourke update the classic satchel with the characteristic hallmarks of an uptown bag: a bamboo handle, safety catch, and little metal feet to protect the underside.

woman is both a weapon and a shield. In it lurks the means for urban and suburban survival and defense, as well as the means for taking the world by storm." The magazine's informal survey revealed that women carry an enormous variety of "useful" objects, including: medication, Band-Aids, an organizer such as Filofax, glasses, tissues, wallet, checkbook, keys, change purse, magazines, paperbacks, socks, sneakers, tights, to-do list, correspondence (in-coming and out-going), stamps, notepad, pens, pencils, receipts, rubber bands, paper clips, gum, candy, breath fresheners, moist towelettes, Mace, whistle, Swiss army knife, tampons, sewing kit, tape measure, gloves, garage door opener, photographs, mirror, cosmetics and cosmetic bag, hand lotion, perfume, comb, brush, barrettes, lighter, matches, cigarettes, ziplock plastic bags (for food), contact lens case and solution, schedules, and maps."[17]

Also a cell phone, beeper, a music system like the Walkman, an electronic organizer, and a miniature camera. Plus water – many women carry a bottle of spring water. Also extra pairs of shoes (many new bags are designed especially to incorporate these), as well as pantyhose, sunglasses, a scarf and/or hat, vitamin C, skin cream, and so on, ad infinitum. Mothers, of course, carry even more paraphernalia: diapers, a bottle, juice, pacifier, snacks, clean clothes, stuffed animal and/or other toys, etc.

The contents of a woman's bag can resemble the Freudian unconscious. Or, as designer Nathalie Hambro says, "A woman carries her neuroses in her handbag."[18] Women do seem to carry objects that calm their insecurities and support their vanity. "I think bringing a salon treatment on the road is a telling sign of insecurity," says producer Cheryl Smith. Then there is "all the other stuff that comes with carrying your stuff," adds television executive Betsy Zeidman. "You know, the stuff below the stuff: frayed business cards, pennies, ancient receipts, tampon wrappers, cigarette tobacco, even though you quit a while ago ..." Despite it all, journalist Betsy Israel probably speaks for many women when she insists that "Purses hold out the hope of a better, or at least a better-arranged, life."[19]

Not only can the contents of a woman's bag be interpreted along Freudian lines, but the bag itself can be seen as symbolic. A recurring trend in contemporary handbag advertising is the prevalence of images of women fighting over bags. This theme has been used in advertising campaigns by Dolce & Gabbana, Francesco Biasia, and Louis Vuitton. Although undoubtedly visually compelling, the meaning of these images is not altogether clear. What does it mean to show one woman pulling another woman's hair while trying to snip the straps of her bag in an attempt to steal it? Are they simply alluding to the possibility that other women will covet an expensive new bag?

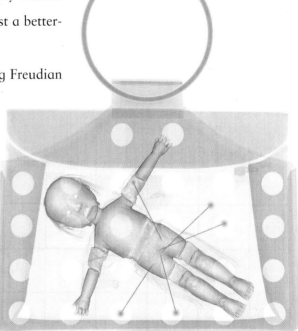

In light of the erotic overtones in these images, it seems more likely that some reference to Freudian symbolism is intended. Freud's most famous book, *The Interpretation of Dreams*, proposed that long and stiff objects (like cigarettes) were phallic symbols, while hollow receptacles were symbols of the

LEFT This game of blind man's bluff is played for high stakes, as the "prize" is a Louis Vuitton Monogram Vernis bag. The stolen bag is a recurrent theme in handbag advertising. Although these images are visually compelling, their meaning is obscure, but it seems likely that some reference to Freudian symbolism is intended. Bags have been interpreted as symbols of the female sex, of the womb, and of (female) vanity and identity.

female genitals.[20] Freud was not the first to make this connection. Indeed, the use of the word "purse" as a slang term for the female pudenda dates from the seventeenth century. The bag has also long been thought of as a symbol of worldly vanity and, in particular, of female vanity. Bags have, on occasion, been interpreted as symbols for the womb.

The bag can also be conceptualized as a kind of miniature house – which is itself a symbol for the body. An advertising campaign for Furla exhorts women to "Bring your world with you." New York designer Tia Wou plays with the idea of the bag as a portable world, naming her line of lightweight tote bags "Tote le Monde." Certainly, women often carry objects that refer to their own world, and they seem to identify with their bags. When asked "what one object do you travel with to make a hotel room your own?" the celebrated architect Zaha Hadid answered: "my handbag."[21] Former British Prime Minister Margaret Thatcher famously referred to her handbag as "my trusty companion."[22] And while the rest of us might never express our relationship with our everyday bag in quite such emotive terms, deep down we know we would be hard-pressed to manage without it.

OPPOSITE Your bag is part of the first impression people make of you. This impression is often based on a practical bag, as it is the most-often carried. Etro's campaign by Michael Wooley features masked models and plays with the question of identity.

BELOW Practical bags are for women on the go. Prada designs a shoulder bag that stands out in the jungle, urban or otherwise. Loud logos are banished and the bag reduced to a streamlined envelope with a long strap which can be slung across the body.

OPPOSITE Practical bags move from the office into the evening, from the gym on to dinner. Here Maurice Scheltens' photograph captures the modern woman's increasingly informal lifestyle.

BELOW Redwall's tote pays tribute to the paper shopping bag. From Harrod's green and gold signature bags to Lord & Taylor's red and white bags, shopping bags have influenced designers, some of whom have recreated them in more durable materials.

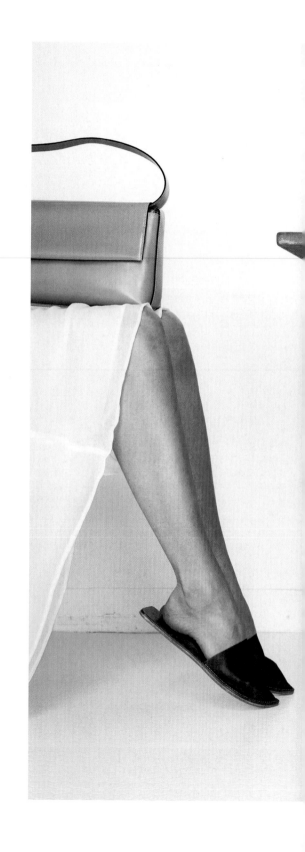

OVERLEAF Leather in all its myriad forms is used to make practical bags. Orla Kiely designed this tote in multi-colored shearling, which allows for a soft construction, while the exposed seams give it a rugged, handmade feeling.

OPPOSITE Sergio Rossi's structured shoulder bag looks sturdy and ultra-modern. This advertising image by Miles Aldrige implies that the bag is designed to weather many storms, while the color, material, and angular body give it a clinical edge.

ABOVE The practical bag is essential to every woman's life, but most of us use it to make a statement in addition to simply carrying around our things. Kenneth Cole's slick red bag grabs attention with its glossy sheen and seductive color.

LEFT Missoni's bags and clothing are made from the same colorful knits. The stripy shoulder bag shown here provides a more affordable fashion fix than a whole ensemble.

ABOVE Inside this East-West shoulder bag by Amy Chan are structured compartments which can be used to separate and organize the contents of your purse.

OPPOSITE The practical bag can be used as a weapon or a shield. Sergio Rossi's bag, with its hard edges, blood-red color, and metallic glint, appears designed to survive a struggle.

ABOVE LEFT & RIGHT Continuing the tradition of creating distinctive luggage for traveling in style, Louis Vuitton updates the travel bag and the hat or bandbox, turning them into much-coveted accessories. A peek of red lingerie hints at the intimate world contained within the bag.

ABOVE Since World War II, when women began to work outside the home on a mass scale, military-inspired shoulder bags have been popular. This modern take on the idea is by Chanel.

RIGHT Etro and paisley are nearly synonymous, and the label's classic range of bags evoke an old-world elegance, as captured here by Christopher Griffith.

OPPOSITE The contents of a woman's bag can resemble the Freudian unconscious. Ines van Lamsweerde hints at the link between the material world and the interior realm in this provocative image for Patrick Cox.

ABOVE Calvin Klein's cK tote has outside pockets for easy access to frequently used items. With its invisible fastenings, pockets, and techno material, it is presented as a hand-held extension of the wearer's jacket, part of the uniform of its owner.

OPPOSITE Men and women have quite different ideas about what is essential. Almost every woman considers her everyday bag to be crucial to her existence, an idea conveyed in this image by Luis Sanchis for Cerruti 1881.

chapter two Precious

precious

"The evening bag you choose makes a statement, but there's nothing more telling about your personality than a peek at the goods inside."[1]

Christine Lennon, Harper's Bazaar

ABOVE Few bag makers epitomize the appeal of the precious aesthetic as Daniel Swarovski does. Only thirty of his bejeweled Balmoral bags were ever made.

OPPOSITE Precious bags hold only what is essential for an evening on the town. This rhinestone-studded bag by Swarovski packs a lot of glamour on its own.

Precious little evening bags have just enough room for a lipstick and mad money. They are as pretty as they are impractical for anything more complicated than a night on the town. Yet these tiny purses – and their contents – potentially reveal a lot about the women who carry them.

The modern It-girl might carry a beaded Fendi Baguette sparkling with rhinestones and flashing its logo. Inside she carries only a few essentials: "No cash (it's on the house); a Mercer hotel room key; M.A.C. lipgloss [and] the new[est] ... cell phone." The downtown girl carries her apartment key and a beeper in a colorful Zoebe bag. The uptown society lady carries her platinum Amex card and a compact in, of course, a Chanel bag, while the fashionista carries the latest Gucci bag containing make-up "snagged from a photo shoot" and Aspégic headache powder.[2]

"All you really need is keys, makeup, and money," says designer Anna Sui, herself a very downtown kind of chick.[3] One does need to ask, though: Which makeup, whose keys, and do you really need money – or is someone else going to foot the bill? What else is defined as essential for an evening out? (That headache medicine sounds ominous.) Most important, how do you choose the bag itself? And what messages does it really convey?

Glamorous evening bags are made of precious materials and feature unique details. Although most ordinary bags are made of leather, precious bags are usually crafted from silk, taffeta, organza, satin, moiré, brocade, faille, muslin, or velvet. Not only are the basic materials luxurious, precious bags also feature jewel-like embellishments. Indeed, these bags are not unlike jewels.

OPPOSITE There is something old-fashioned about evening bags.
Shalom Harlow poses gracefully for Nick Knight – in her gloved
hand she holds a tiny bag by Christian Dior, recalling a bygone era.

"The handbag can play the role of jewelry in complementing an outfit," says Christian Lacroix, whose own bags are characterized by couture-quality attention to detail.[4] Precious bags often feature hand-beading, sequins or embroidery. A Jamin Puech evening bag might be made of tulle reembroidered with sequins, for example, or a Daniel Swarovski bag covered with hand-cut Austrian crystals. Moreover, just as different kinds of jewelry convey very different style messages – grandmother's pearls versus a coiled metal "tribal" necklace by John Galliano – so also do different bags.

The classic evening bag of the 1950s was made of black satin or black velvet, often enlivened with rhinestones. The very rich could buy such bags with eighteen-carat gold frames set in diamonds. Indeed, in the past wealthy women often carried bags made of precious materials – gold, silver, ivory, leopard skin – and all of the great jewelers have made evening bags decorated with precious or semi-precious stones. But the appeal of the evening bag is not dependent on either famous names (Fendi, Gucci) or the incorporation of expensive materials (Austrian crystal, jewels). Both status and luxury are desirable, of course, but are ultimately less important than artistry and charm.

The definitive characteristic of precious bags is their size. A very small bag implies that the woman is being taken care of, like the Queen of England (who famously never carries any money). There is snob appeal in smallness. As style-icon Blaine Trump observes, "You just want evening bags to disappear and be objects of amusement."[5] Precious bags are the antithesis of the practical, every-day survival kit. They are "anti-schlep" bags.[6] Indeed, they are conspicuously

ABOVE This Jamin Puech wristlet is made of richly embroidered fabrics. Wristlets are usually designed with a handle at the top center, which ensures that the weight of the bag is even as it dangles daintily from the wrist.

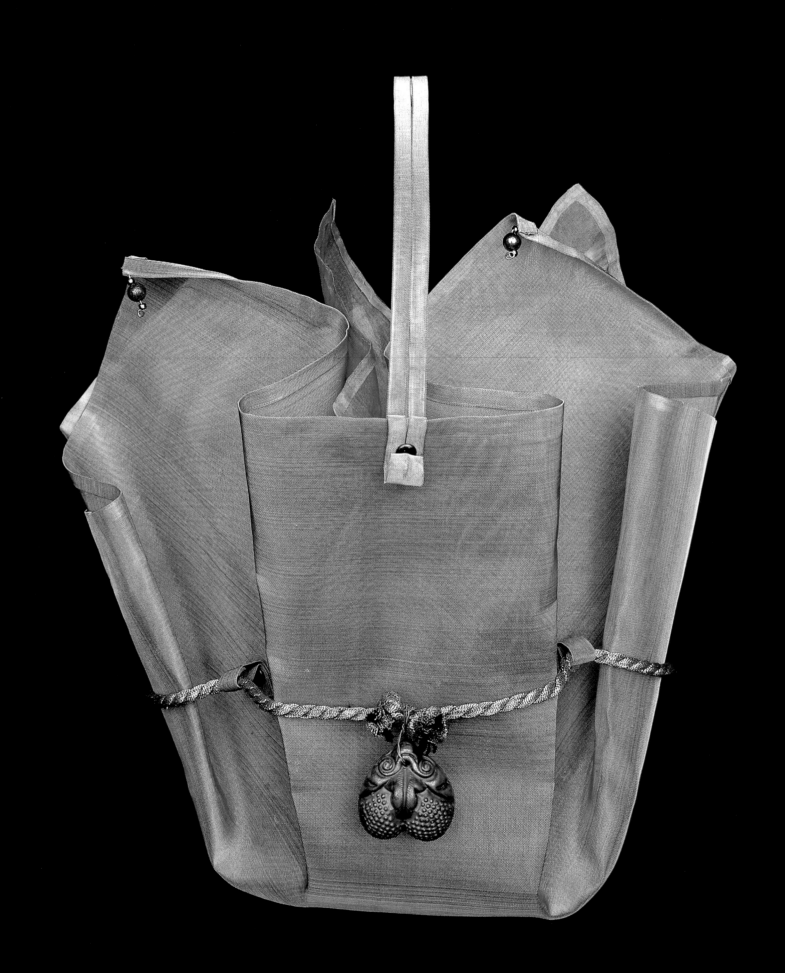

"high maintenance" bags – akin to the "limousine shoes" worn by women who don't need to walk far. Purses of this sort include Lambertson Truex's small satin Stiletto bag and thin Satin Swagger clutch, as well as Swarovski's delicate beaded pouches with silk-satin linings.

Vogue Italia compares the bags of Ikuko Akatsuka to bonsai – the miniaturized trees characteristic of Japanese gardening. According to *Vogue*, these "borsetta" are like little sculptures.[7] At its best, the evening bag resembles a bibelot, having both visual and tactile appeal (and very little utility). "You can place your bag on the table, on display – like an object," says designer Nathalie Hambro.[8]

The tiny handbag, like Cinderella's shoe, represents femininity, so perhaps it implies that women are smaller – and weaker – than men. A woman clutching a little beaded purse does send a different sexual message from the woman with a big, structured alligator bag, which might be used as a weapon.

In her book *Bags and Purses*, Vanda Foster reports that "in 1952, a woman who complained that tiny evening bags would not hold both cosmetics and a cigarette case was told that 'any woman smart enough to carry this tiny handbag is sure of an escort who will provide the cigarettes.'"[9] Cigarettes may be out of fashion today, but cosmetics are always mentioned in connection with evening bags. They are perhaps the only essential items that a male escort could not be expected to provide for a woman in the course of an evening, and so the evening bag shrinks to a size just large enough to contain them. In this

ABOVE Precious bags are often decorated with delicate and feminine iconography. This bag by Christian Lacroix is embellished with hand-painted flowers and a jeweled ornament.

DANIEL SWAROVSKI
—— P A R I S ——

ABOVE Beading is a popular type of ornamentation for precious bags. Swarovski is famous for its Austrian crystals, here strung into a web-like pouch lined with silk.

OPPOSITE Desmo's sweet posy of a bag, called Eden, demonstrates why flowers are a popular style of decoration for precious bags. They convey an immediate impression of delicate femininity, and, in this case especially, luxuriant beauty.

sense the evening bag emphasizes the woman's decorative and dependent role at evening social events.

An evening bag is "like a tabernacle," says François Lesage, owner of the famous Parisian embroidery business. "It's where women put the sacraments to make their beauty more so."[10] Beauty is obviously important to many women, and the belief that cosmetics make them more beautiful has made the cosmetics industry extremely successful. Yet cosmetics – and especially lipstick – also create an artificial mask that signifies the triumph of erotic femininity and defies the ravages of time and death. The purse may not be a tabernacle, but applying lipstick can be a ritual act.

In the 1920s many evening bags were little more than rigid vanity cases for make-up. Some of the prettiest were made in France in new materials such as celluloid, a kind of plastic that could be moulded into various shapes with internal compartments for lipstick, rouge, and powder. Tiny lipstick-shaped reticules were not much larger than the lipsticks themselves. They dangled on long chains or silk cords, or were attached to round bangles and worn on the wrist. One novelty bag of 1921 was shaped like a doll, with the skirt forming

ABOVE Designers can easily experiment with the shape and embellishment of precious bags because they serve occasion-specific needs, unlike practical bags, which are all-purpose. Philip Treacy's bag is paisley-shaped and has a beaded handle.

the purse. For better or for worse, there is something old-fashioned about evening bags, which are directly descended from the reticule of 1800. They are the opposite of utility bags, and thus convey an image of women as being somehow helpless dolls – were it not for the power of their beauty.

As tiny as toys, precious bags are often characterized by delicate, overtly "feminine" iconography. Flowers in particular are a recurring and popular motif. "Sometimes an evening bag looks for all the world like a bunch of violets but its stems pull apart and leave just enough room for a bit of rouge and powder and a handkerchief like a cobweb," observed *Vogue* in 1921.[11]

Schiaparelli designed bags shaped like flower pots, and sixty years later Lulu Guinness – who Lucy Sykes of *Allure* calls "the Blahnik of bags" – also created a bucket bag blooming with roses. She has subsequently made a number of different versions of the Flower Pot.[12] Nathalie Hatgis, whose Violette Nozières floral bags are conceived of within the context of "a romantic ideal

within the framework of distinct modernism," describes her floral designs with sophisticated poetry: "The nascent bud in hand-tinted organza, the wandering tendril of an embossed velvet leaf."[13] Kazuyo Nakano also often adorns her bags with hand-embroidered flowers. She believes that feminism is changing and that the women who buy "lady bags" are "comfortable to be feminine without feeling the need to compete with men like in the eighties."[14] Rafé Totengco's straw basket bag embroidered with purple velvet Czechoslovakian pansies pleased his Japanese customers, who thought the flowers were cute.[15]

The iconography associating women with flowers goes back many centuries and crosses many cultures. Flowers are the sex organs of plants, and women have always traditionally been linked to sex and fertility. Also, because flowers usually bloom in spring, they are associated with new beginnings, and with the fleeting beauty of youth.

Evening bags are almost always held in the hand, although sometimes they dangle from the wrist, hang on a delicate necklace-like chain, or are clutched under the arm. They have an especially intimate physical relationship with the woman who carries them, since only one of her hands is really free. Since these bags are often quite valuable, most women probably prefer to hold onto them – but they are undeniably impractical. Like the fan, though, the evening bag serves to call attention to the hand that holds it, placing a premium on satin skin, slim wrists, a perfect manicure, and lovely jewels.

Evening bags, like evening dresses, are often marked by an element of fantasy. Not only their decoration, but even their shapes can be whimsical.

OPPOSITE & LEFT A simple shell, when held up to the ear, reveals the sound of the sea. This shell bag, by Dolce & Gabbana, opens to a roar. The lining is a leopard print, the glamour of which contrasts with the simple, craft-like decoration of the bag's body, to which shells are crocheted.

This is particularly so with *minaudières* which often take on the form of plants and animals. *Minaudières* are small cases that combine the functions of purse and compact. It is popularly held that Charles Arpel designed the first *minaudière* in 1933 after observing the socialite Florence Jay Gould carrying her makeup and lighter in a metal Lucky Strikes cigarette case.[16] In her book on bags, Claire Wilcox reports that Alfred Van Cleef patented the name as "a tribute to his wife Estelle, who had a tendency to *minauder*, meaning to simper or charm."[17] Designers from Cartier to Calvin Klein have since made sleek and geometric *minaudières*, but Judith Leiber's name is synonymous with jeweled *minaudières* in amusing shapes, such as a sleeping cat or a tomato, the latter covered with thousands of red crystals. Each bag requires three to seven days to make, because it is sculpted in wax, cast in metal, and gold-plated, at which point some 7,000 rhinestones or crystals are hand-set over a painted design.

Wristlets are another type of evening bag which combine the functions of purse and jewelry, slipping around the wrist like a bracelet. Cloisonné bracelets form the handle of Amy Chan's Chinese-inspired wrist bags. Wristlets with straps, such as Anya Hindmarch's beige satin beaded model or Chanel's circle

BELOW Philip Treacy has applied his milliner's sensibilities to a two-tone sculptural leather bag. This unconventional design has an ovoid shape, and the handle is one with the bag.

ABOVE One of the most popular types of evening bag is the mini-tote with handles. This glowing example in silver leather is by London designer Bill Amberg.

RIGHT Judith Leiber's name has become synonymous with *minaudières* made in amusing shapes, to resemble a tomato or a polar bear, for example. Each of the thousands of tiny rhinestones that cover these bags is set by hand.

OPPOSITE The clutch or *pochette* first became popular in the early twentieth century. Although its origins are practical, it is typically used as an evening bag, as its slim shape generally allows for only limited contents. Here, Sonia Rykiel gives the clutch a modern, mannish appeal, as photographed by Mario Testino.

of ivory felt camellias, are designed with the wrist strap at the center top of the bag, so that the bag can dangle in a balanced manner. Some women like wristlets, because it is not always safe to leave a bag unattended while dancing.

The clutch, or *pochette*, was introduced in 1916. It is a slim rectangular bag that combines the cool efficiency of an envelope or portfolio with the elegance of a precious bag. "Attached directly to the hand it was expressive in the same way as the fan or the cigarette. Tucked under the arm it gave a military hauteur, or, balanced against the hip, an air of nonchalant chic."[18] The popularity of the clutch in the 1950s was perhaps as a reaction against the shoulder bags of the war, but it has often been revived. It was popular in the seventies, when its minimal lines could resemble a portfolio or a rolled-up magazine. Lulu Guinness now makes a clutch in the shape of a flat, open fan.

Small bags with handles are currently the most popular type of evening bag. The handles themselves are often delicate, pretty, and highly decorative, recalling necklaces and lingerie straps. James Coviello's miniature leopard tote for evening has fuschia velvet and floral jacquard ribbon straps. Vintage ribbons and flowers add a romantic touch. Handles can also be made to resemble tortoiseshell or amber. Chain straps can be as pretty as necklaces, or beaded with baubles. Satin ribbons can lend a lingerie appeal. Patch NYC's tiny pouches are decorated with small embroidered and beaded motifs. The frame bag also utilizes a wide range of decorative materials. Frames are usually hinged at either side so that they open like jaws from the top. A fabric, leather, or mesh pouch is attached to the frame,

BELOW *Minaudières*, like this one by Rodo, combine the functions of purse and compact. They became popular in the twenties and thirties when wearing cosmetics became generally accepted.

LEFT The It-girl and the uptown woman carry different types of bags that reveal their different characters and lifestyles. Etro offers choices to tempt every woman, from classic to chic to cool.

BELOW French design duo Jamin Puech are renowned for their exquisitely beaded and sequinned bags. They named the Gloria bag after an imaginary saloon dancer, whose corseted body is conjured up in the bag's skeleton of draped and glistening strings.

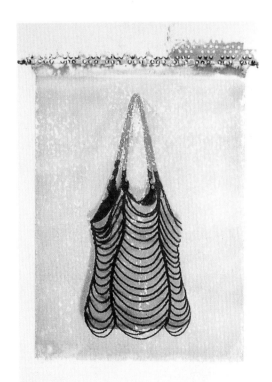

which usually has a chain handle. Instead of a frame, Dorothy bags have a drawstring closure.

Many contemporary evening bags deliberately recall the styles of the past. Laura Bortolami, for example, designs mesh bags of "liquid metal" that evoke the glamour of the jazz age. Orla Kiely makes what she calls "granny bags" with exposed gold metal frames and colorful bodies. Audrey Ang uses vintage seventies fabrics in her designs, and Sarah Violet makes "one-of-a-kind" bags using vintage embroidered table linens.

Fabric is enticingly tactile. More malleable than leather, fabric lends itself to embellishment. Bindya Lulla created an entire collection of bags using antique sari fabrics and vintage Kashmiri embroidered shawls. Lustrous and luxurious fabrics, such as silks and satins, taffetas, organzas, brocades and jacquards, velvets and failles, organdy and lace, also carry feminine associations, especially in the industrialized West, where men long ago retreated into sober uniformity.

Beading is the most popular type of embellishment lavished on small evening bags. French *Vogue* asserts that a beaded bag adds a "luminous touch against a black dress for an important evening, a note of color against a beige cashmere for day. Little beaded bags are the new fantasy."[19] Matthew Williamson's hand-beaded bags are popular with fashion editors and models such as Naomi Campbell. Hand-beading with sequins and beads can be used to

ABOVE Ribbons and flowers lend a romantic touch to James Coviello's mini-tote. Precious bags like this are used more and more during the day, rather than just for evenings, to bring individuality to the modern fashion uniform of chromatic colors.

vintage or contemporary effect. Jamin Puech bags, designed by Isabelle Jamin and Benoît Puech in France, have attained a cult following. *The New Yorker* compared them to "artistic handbag[s] that Vanessa Bell might have brought back as a souvenir of her 1906 trip to Constantinople."[20] Other beaded bags have been described as "one part Jazz Age, two parts Y2K (year 2000),"[21] because they combine retro styling with the latest contemporary fashion trends.

The Constellation bag from Violette Nozières combines jewelry-making techniques, metal weaving, and semi-precious stones like quartz, carnelian, and citrine. This rectangular bag is constructed from sterling silver jeweler's wire that catches and suspends semi-precious stones in the wire as if they were stars. The look is deliberately "rough, raw, and ragged," says the designer, who aimed to combine the beauty of tribalism and femininity. Much beadwork is done by hand. It takes an artisan eight hours to make a single Bottega Veneta evening bag decorated with hand-strung glass beads. Erickson Beamon, known for their "Cinderella fantasies," also make bags that are extremely labor intensive, sometimes incorporating beads made of semi-precious stones.

Besides beading and embroidery, bag designers often use knitting and crochet techniques. Irish crocheted bags were very popular in the 1900s paired with summery lawn dresses. Today, Lorenzo Gandaglia makes hand-crocheted

OPPOSITE The Safar Wreath shoulder bag and the Putau wristlet by Zoebe have a lot of "ethno glam." They are made of Indian sari fabric from Madras and are embellished with beading. Zoebe bags are fashionable among the young and hip.

BELOW Laura B manipulates the most delicate and romantic of fabrics, lace, into a spare, minimal shape which is enticingly tactile. She also plays with the see-through quality of lace.

ABOVE Walter Steiger's metallic leather handbag has a mercury-like surface and a Mobius-strip of a handle. Silver is associated with high-tech and is often used by designers to express the idea of effervescent modernity.

OPPOSITE Precious bags are not unlike jewels. The Constellation bag by Violette Nozières features semi-precious stones including quartz, rose quartz, and moonstones. The bag was constructed by hand using jewelry-making techniques and was intended to have a raw rather than a finished feeling.

bags, some decorated with Kachina dolls. The English designer Jo Gordon creates colorful knitted bags, as does Petro Zillia, who combines mohair and beads. Céia Crema uses knotting techniques, like those used in rug-making, to turn fabric strips into vibrant bags that she describes as "the perfect accessory to go with black."[22] British *Elle* approvingly described the look of "naive folksy embroidery" as "part Arts and Crafts movement, part Woodstock."[23]

Ethnically-inspired bags are often popular. In the 1920s the discovery of Tutenkahmen's tomb sparked Egyptomania, while designers like Paul Poiret mixed references from the Near and Far East. Multiculturalism is once again an important theme, especially in fashion. Karin Zoebelin says that color is a major part of the "ethno-glam" appeal of her Zoebe line. She started designing bags after her own was stolen, and her first inspiration was a piece of sari fabric produced in Madras for the West African market.[24] Daphna Dor of Chista often designs bags with an ethnic flair. Some of her bags are made in Indonesia out of hand-cut and beaded pieces of fish vertebrae. Sara Hatchuel, who with Sasha Berry designs the Aatou line of bags using traditional Asian fabrics, says: "These days it's modern to mix cultures."[25] Indeed, the predictions for the turn of the millennium are for an "ethnic luxe." According to British *Vogue*, what works is a "subtle fusion of references." [26]

Perhaps the essence of the precious evening bag is its handwork, which gives it an artistic and personal quality. In the past, satin evening bags were often dyed to coordinate with a particular evening ensemble. But today *Vogue* says: "Should the words 'Coordinate your purse with pumps' set off a flashback to

ABOVE Precious bags are the most feminine of bags, designed to hold only keys, some mad money, and cosmetics. This sequinned mini-tote by Prada, as photographed by Astrid Zuidema, is tempting "arm candy" with its lollipop pink color and sparkling surface.

Emily Post, ignore it! After all, rules aren't made to be broken – they're made to be beaded, embroidered, and bejeweled."[27] Both decorative and personal, evening bags reveal something of a woman's fantasies and wishes. As Claire Wilcox puts it: "Ever since the handbag became an essential accessory, evening bags have provided the element of fantasy and indulgence missing from more functional day bags."[28]

It is also important to recognize that today precious bags are not just used in the evening. They also bring a fantasy element to daytime ensembles, which have tended to become increasingly bland and minimal. Many women now choose to pair precious bags with relaxed, plain clothing as a mark of individuality. Unexpected juxtapositions – such as a beaded bag with jeans or a delicately embroidered purse with business attire – play with traditional conventions of appropriate dress. They can add an element of whimsy or irony, or even express a woman's personal fantasies.

RIGHT The louder the click of a frame bag snapping closed, the higher its quality. These leather bags by Roberta di Camerino are named "Chopin" and "Liszt." Designer Guiliana Camerino is influenced by nineteenth-century doctor's bags and jewelry cases.

ABOVE Louis Vuitton transforms the vanity case in Monogram Vernis into precious cargo. The antithesis of practical bags, precious bags support a woman's beauty for an evening. Their smallness suggests that a woman is somehow being taken care of.

OPPOSITE Daphna Dor, co-founder of Chista, is inspired by traditional methods of craftsmanship and unusual materials. This fishbone bag with crystal handles was made in Indonesia, where each tiny piece was hand-cut and beaded.

OPPOSITE & ABOVE A loaded bag? Tanner Krolle's witty

advertising campaign plays with perception and reality. Its series

of X-rayed bags reveal surprising contents – in this case a water

pistol is concealed in what seems to be a very lady-like beaded

bag. At the same time, its shimmering gunmetal color and covering

of tiny beaded scales gives it a distinctly modern edge. The bag is

a collector's item, each bead stitched on by hand.

ABOVE Kirsten Owen is photographed by Karl Lagerfeld
with a Fendi bag which is romantically embellished with a fringe.
Glamorous evening bags are made of precious materials and
feature unique details, such as fringing, which languorously sways
as the wearer moves about.

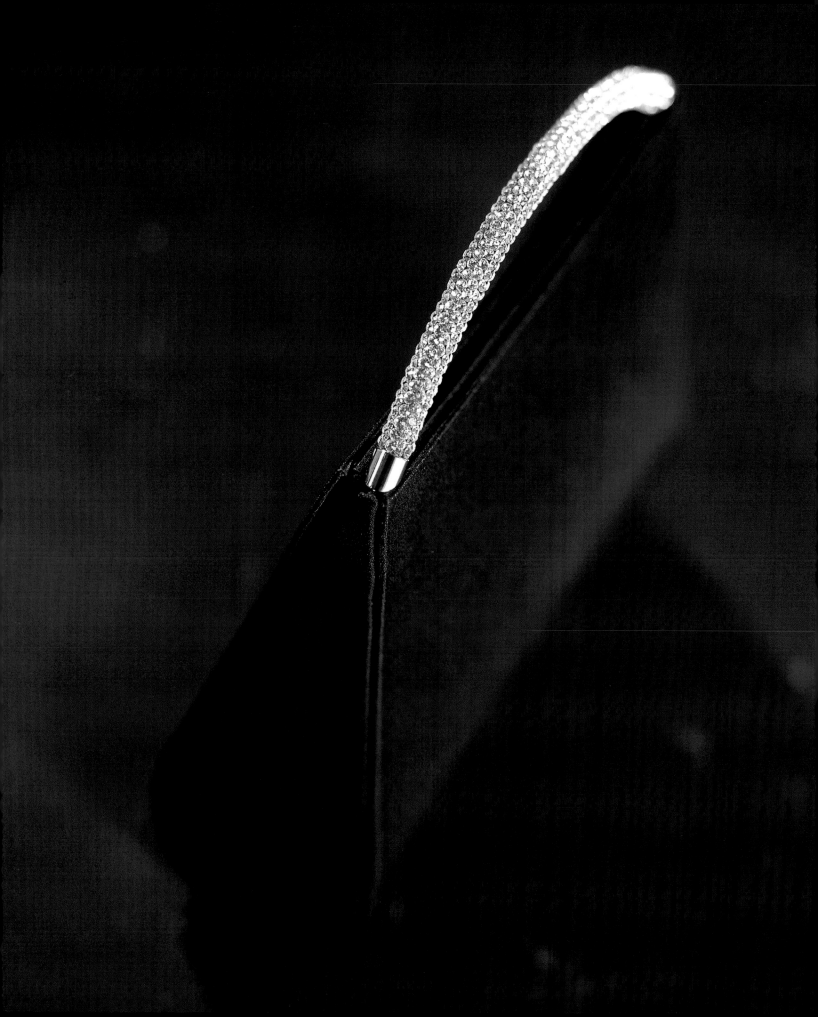

LEFT & BELOW Striking a precious pose for a precious bag by Etro. The model's stance suggests the delicacy of the bag and implies its role as fetish object. Sonia Rykiel's East-West bag, meanwhile, is styled to emphasize its sex appeal.

OPPOSITE Precious bags are characteristically tiny. In fact there is a snob appeal in smallness, as exemplified in Daniel Swarovski's black satin envelope, which evokes classic glamour. The handle is encrusted in a mosaic of crystals.

OPPOSITE Precious bags are often characterized by delicate and overtly feminine iconography, such as flowers. Rafé's straw tote is embroidered with summer blooms. Rafé Totengco approaches the design process from the perspective that it is "serious fun."

RIGHT Clutches, like fans, are hand-held. Appropriately, Lulu Guinness' clutch is designed in the shape of an open fan and is as coquettish as that now-forgotten accessory.

LEFT Practical bags are often described as portable offices or homes. Lulu Guinness humorously transforms a precious bag into a portable cottage, flanked here by her signature flowerpot bags.

ABOVE LEFT & RIGHT Two tiny bags that are equally feminine, but in different ways: Desmo's rose and feather pouch is conventionally pretty, while Céia Crema's woven bag is naive in its appeal. Soft knit and crochet bags often seem feminine as these arts are usually considered to be "women's work."

RIGHT The colors and crafts of India inspired this bag by Bazar de Christian Lacroix. It is made of raw silk and is ornamented with mirrors, buttons, and multi-colored beads.

OPPOSITE This wristlet was designed by Mari Aoyama and resembles a tiny nest. Its three-dimensionality and delicacy are striking and command attention. It is truly a high-maintenance bag.

BELOW Amy Chan's wristlet combines the roles of jewelry and handbag. For the handles of this metallic knitted bag, the designer – who characteristically employs Asian fabrics and decorative devices – has used Chinese red lacquer bracelets.

OPPOSITE Perhaps the essence of the precious bag is its handwork. Hand-beading and embroidery on a velvet background distinguish this beautiful, unusually shaped Etro bag in the Chinoiserie style, photographed by Christopher Griffith.

OPPOSITE Women often hold on tightly to their precious bags, which are "anti-schlep" but also highly interactive. As tiny as toys, they seem to demand to be touched, coddled, and cosseted, as this image from Missoni conveys.

BELOW An element of fantasy unites a woman to her precious bag like no other, as Jason Tanaka Blaney's photograph shows us. Vintage or of-the-moment, precious bags are delightful adornments. And, like Cinderella, they usually go out only at night.

chapter three Status

status

"Naomi Campbell steps from her Mercedes ... and carries a Vuitton box."[1]

Philip Weiss, Vogue

ABOVE Different types of status bags appeal to different style tribes. This sleek Cartier vanity bag is for the woman who sees the Cartier label as a badge testifying to her refined taste.

OPPOSITE Status bags combine quality and cachet as Kareem Iliya demonstrates in his illustration of a Louis Vuitton Damier bag, instantly recognizable by its brown and gold checkerboard pattern.

Status symbols, like the Mercedes automobile and the Louis Vuitton bag, are objects to which a set of unspoken but powerful associations is attached. The logo is like a license plate that announces: "We're from the same tribe."[2] Or at least we have the same credit limit.

A vintage Hermès bag can sell at auction for $10,000.[3] Louis Vuitton's colorful Vernis patent leather handbags, designed by Marc Jacobs, rang up sales of $40 million during the first nine months they were available. The pink Murray backpack, which retails for $1,060, has been the hottest single item worldwide since its launch in 1999.[4] Clearly, the status bag has a powerful appeal. But why? According to journalist Vicki Woods, it is "the smell of money. Few of us are immune."[5] However, this raises as many questions as it answers. After all, it is circular logic to argue that a status bag is worth big money, because people will pay big money for it. Or is it? Perhaps Alice-in-Wonderland logic is the only kind that can explain why objects with certain logos are the fix of the label junkie, who firmly believes that they provide "instant cool and fashion pedigree."[6]

It is almost always possible to find a good "knock-off" of a status bag. Indeed, the companies that produce status bags spend considerable time and effort trying to crack down on the many cheap imitations that flood the market worldwide. Yet, despite the plethora of inexpensive copies, many people are reluctant to buy an imitation designer bag. As Marina Rust writes in *Vogue*: "What does it say about me, as a person, if I carry a knock-off?"[7] Presumably it implies that you, too, are a fake.

BELOW & OPPOSITE The Chanel 2005 – only time will tell whether it has the staying power of its predecessor the ubiquitous 2.55, commonly known as the "gilt 'n' quilt" bag, which has endured since 1955. Modern status seekers may well turn to the 2005, as much for its high-tech looks and indestructible appearance as for the fact that everyone will know it cost a lot.

Fashion experts tend to suspect that women will pay big money for a "label" bag – like Louis Vuitton, Gucci, or Chanel – because it is "a security blanket." As Betty Halbreich writes in her book *Secrets of a Fashion Therapist*, "By carrying a recognizable name brand, you're announcing your good taste (and maybe wealth) to everyone you pass on the street. Now of course I'm not trying to suggest that the only reason women buy expensive bags is that they're insecure. Spending a lot on a bag buys you much more than status."[8]

It also buys quality, since status bags are usually handcrafted and made of luxurious materials. Yet, ultimately, the appeal of the status bag depends on more intangible qualities. A Gucci bag, for example, comes with the related glamour portrayed in the advertisements. Status bags combine quality and cachet. They offer associative glamour through the logo or the *griffe*.

Griffe is a French word meaning claw or talon, and, by extension, mark or logo. The animal quality of clawing or imprinting a mark upon something is resonant, as if the association of the status bag marks the wearer out of the crowd. In the past, members of the ruling class often had their own symbols, colors, or monograms attached to objects they owned, and even to people who worked for them. In the modern era, a host of ordinary people also sought to distinguish themselves through the use of elite symbolism. At first this was done in imitation of European aristocrats, as, for example, when wealthy commoners invented spurious coats of arms. Later, as advanced capitalism evolved, certain consumer goods began to acquire prestige of a rather different kind.

Now it was not enough to have one's own monogram embroidered on, say, shirts, slips, and tablecloths. It was also perceived as prestigious to buy certain goods, which carried their own identifying marks.

"Monogram mania" exploded in the 1980s when conspicuous consumption was the order of the day. Yet, already by the 1950s and 1960s, wealthy trendsetters were covering themselves with fashionable logos: Hermès scarves, Gucci loafers, and so on. But what gives a particular bag cult status? According to one branding expert, a cult bag must have the following three characteristics: 1) "legitimacy within the fashion industry, 2) great advertising, and 3) celebrity support."[9] The first of these is, perhaps, the most important – or, at least, the hardest to fake, since it implies a history of excellence and prestige. Traditionally, within the fashion world, the greatest prestige has accrued to certain couture houses.

It is not surprising, therefore, that the quilted Chanel bag with the braided gold chain handle is, arguably, *the* status bag of all time. Mademoiselle Gabrielle Chanel (1883-1971), known as Coco Chanel, is widely regarded as the most important fashion designer of the twentieth century. A recognized fashion trendsetter at the beginning of the century, even before she began designing clothes, Chanel was her own best model. When she bobbed her hair, got a suntan, and wore costume jewelry mixed in among her fabulous real

jewels, other women noticed and followed suit. In 1955, Chanel designed her first quilted handbag with a gilt chain, which she named the "2.55," after the month and the year of its introduction. It was made in Chanel's favorite colors of beige, navy, black, and brown and came in a choice of two materials: leather or jersey. The chain handles, braided with leather, allowed the bag to be hung over the shoulder, leaving the hands free, in keeping with Chanel's overall philosophy of design, which emphasized functionalism and mobility. The double Cs were added later, but they were congruent with the power of her name.

During the 1950s, fashion was changing rapidly, and Chanel offered women a sensible uniform. In place of Dior's fluctuating A-line and H-line and Y-line, Chanel provided simple, yet expensive tweed suits with cardigan jackets. Flattened gilt chains were sewn into the linings of her suit jackets, to keep them hanging neatly. Some of her jackets also featured quilted linings, in imitation of the quilted jackets worn by stable boys at the races. Her quilted handbag, therefore, derived its notable characteristics from her clothes.

Popularly referred to as the "gilt 'n' quilt" bag, the 2.55 bag continued to sell after Chanel's death in 1971 – although the Chanel style in general became outmoded. It was only when the House of Chanel hired Karl Lagerfeld in 1983 that the Chanel name once more became highly fashionable. Just as Lagerfeld modernized the Chanel suit for a new generation, so also did he modify many of the classic Chanel accessories. He reintroduced the 2.55 in both classic and trendy forms, enlarging the double Cs and tweaking the traditional shape. Once Lagerfeld had renewed the prestige of the House of Chanel, the signature bag

TOP LEFT & ABOVE The Chanel bag has been reworked by Karl Lagerfeld in numerous guises. Whether tiny trapezoids or a calfskin "gilt 'n' quilt," each is identifiable as a Chanel by one or more of the label's status signatures: quilting, gilt logo, and chain strap.

OPPOSITE The sharp, geometric lines and gleaming leather finish of this bag marks it out to knowing fashion followers as by classic French couture house Celine, even without a visible logo.

BELOW Even minus the logo of interlocked Cs and the gilt chain, this bag is instantly recognizable as a Chanel because of the quilting, a characteristic, too, of chic Chanel suits.

was transformed into a symbol of upward mobility. During the 1980s, the power of the double Cs was such that some stores limited customers to three purchases at a time. Barbara Cirkva, senior vice president of fashion at Chanel Inc., affirms that "Chanel dominated the bag market in the eighties."[10]

Now the "gilt 'n' quilt" is regarded as an "establishment" bag, associated with ladies who lunch. Journalist Janet Street-Porter describes eating out at a restaurant where "women kept arriving in mink, with blond streaks and gold jewelry, and all the handbags except mine had gold chains."[11] However, as the 1980s slip further into the past, the stigma associated with that decade's status symbols will fade, and the 2.55 bag may once again come into its own.

Chanel recently launched the 2005 bag, intended as the new Chanel status bag, or in Lagerfeld's words, "the first of the next generation of bags." The 2005 is a modern, futuristic companion to the classic 2.55 and, potentially, the "ultimate accomplice of the twenty-first century woman."[12] Like 2.55, 2005 is a number with meaning. The numeral two indicates that it was designed two years before the millennium. The double zeroes signify the international calling code. The five, of course, was Chanel's lucky number.

The frame of the bag is made of injected polyethylene, covered in leather, tweed, or jersey (to coordinate with Chanel suits). It opens "like one of Lagerfeld's fans" with the CC logo "discreetly" placed on the discs on either side of the bag. Inside there are eight mesh compartments, including a special pocket for a mobile phone with corset-style lacing that accommodates different models and sizes. Chanel describes this "bio-designed" bag as a pebble, but it

BELOW LEFT Even the humble tote becomes a status bag when designed by Cartier, adopting the associated allure of the jewelry maker's name. Made from leather which is hand-polished and glazed, the bags have braided handles that can be worn short or pulled to their full length and worn over the shoulder.

has also been described as a bean, a pear, a tool kit, and "the handbag that thinks it's a BMW."[13]

Like the house of Chanel, Gucci has a distinguished history. In the 1920s the Florentine workshop of Guccio Gucci was producing fine leather luggage. After World War II, when leather was in short supply, the double-G motif was printed on canvas, and it wasn't long before this logo, together with Gucci's signature red and green stripes, became internationally famous. In addition to producing leather goods, the company expanded its range to a variety of licenses, including those for clothing and household items. Ultimately, this expansion cheapened the company's image. As Yves Saint Laurent's partner Pierre Bergé observed, "A name is like a cigarette – the more you puff on it, the less you have left."[14] Another problem was the vast number of Gucci imitations sold worldwide, which reportedly cost the company a fortune in legal fees. The Gucci family was also known for its internal conflicts.

Certain Gucci products, such as the Gucci loafer, were best sellers for many years. But, by the 1980s, the company's problems had eroded much of its prestige. Things only began to improve in 1989, when an American retail executive, Dawn Mello, was appointed creative director of the company. She immediately began to cut back licensing and to edit the core collection of leather accessories, drawing on Gucci's historic archives, while also introducing new fashionable styles.

Designer Tom Ford joined Gucci in 1992, and since then the company can hardly keep up with the demand for its bags and shoes and sexy clothes. Ford's achievement has been to edit and streamline classic Gucci designs and signatures: the double Gs, the horse bits, the red and green webbing, the bamboo handles – and imbue them with sex appeal. The bamboo-handled bag that was designed in 1957, for example, was restyled by Ford in 1995 in metallic patent leather. The Jackie bag (named for Jacqueline Kennedy Onassis) was given new life for spring 1999 in gold metallic leather and neon-bright colors. According to fashion writer Mimi Spencer, "The common thread is that the hot potato accessories are usually from Italy and mostly from Gucci."[15]

Gucci's bags have fashion's imprimatur, but their appeal is widespread. Ford has married sex appeal to design, while drawing on the traditional allure

ABOVE Not all status bags are by European designers nor come with outrageous price tags. Coach bags have gained a following for their understated American looks.

of Italian leather goods. He has also created provocative advertising images. The result is product envy that translates into waiting lists and big money.

Hermès bags also have an illustrious pedigree. The French company was founded in 1837 by Thierry Hermès, a harness and saddle maker. By the 1880s, the company was based in premises on the fashionable rue Faubourg Saint Honoré in Paris. As automobiles replaced horses, Hermès began to produce other leather goods, such as wallets and handbags. Since the 1930s, Hermès has produced a number of classic bag designs, including the famous "small tall bag with straps," which was introduced in 1935. It was renamed the Kelly bag in 1956, when the actress Grace Kelly (Princess Grace of Monaco) appeared on the cover of *Life* magazine carrying the bag.

The association with Grace Kelly illustrates the enduring power of celebrity endorsement. The Kelly bag is still Hermès' top seller. Also popular is the roomy and durable Birkin bag, which was introduced in 1984 after the chairman of Hermès, Jean-Louis Dumas-Hermès, shared a flight with actress Jane Birkin.

Hermès bags have history and character. The company has always closely controlled the production of its goods and has avoided licensing. In addition to leather goods, the Hermès name adorns fourteen other product families, from

ABOVE LEFT Photographer Rudy Faccin von Steidl captured this pink jersey 2005 bag by Chanel on the runway. It has bonsai proportions and hovers closely about the body.

OPPOSITE Celebrity endorsement has helped the Kelly Bag, named after Grace Kelly, achieve iconic status. It came to fame in 1956 when the actress-turned-princess was snapped using the bag to shield her pregnant belly from the prying eyes of the paparazzi. Throughout the 1950s and 1960s other celebrities such as Ingrid Bergman and Marlene Dietrich also carried Hermès bags.

tableware to ready-to-wear. The company is still based in Paris, and has its own museum. Jean-Louis Dumas of Hermès once described the Hermès field bag as being "useful in its elegance and elegant in its utility."[16] These characteristics are also applicable to Hermès' most recent design: the Herbag, which is designed in two modular parts and can be taken apart and put back together. The top is leather and the removable body, which comes in different sizes, is canvas. The frame is made of nickel. Integrating innovation and tradition, this "do-it-yourself handbag" sold out of the Paris store in three days.

Louis Vuitton is a French luggage and accessory firm, established in Paris in 1854. The company's eponymous founder, Louis Vuitton, had trained as a luggage packer for the best Parisian families. Indeed, he was appointed by the Emperor of France, Napoleon III, to pack the dresses of the Empress Eugénie. Having learned about packing, he then went on to design and make luggage, introducing innovations such as flat trunks that could be stacked in railway carriages. As Vuitton's luggage was imitated by other firms, he responded by creating distinctive striped and checkerboard designs.

Louis Vuitton's city bags were derived from their luggage. Some travel bags have become popular handbag styles, like the Noé bag, which was originally designed in 1932 to tote five bottles of champagne. Similarly, the Epi leather collection took its inspiration from leathers used by the firm in the 1920s.

When these patterns also were imitated, he introduced in 1896 his famous Monogram design, which consists of the intersecting LV initials and a curved beige diamond with a four-point star inset and its negative, a beige circle with a four-leafed flower inset. Both the Monogram and Damier (a checkerboard pattern that was launched in 1888 and reintroduced in 1996) collections are today made from a PVC-coated fabric which is embossed with the design.

Just as Tom Ford joined Gucci, so also did fellow American designer Marc Jacobs join Louis Vuitton in 1996. Jacobs redesigned the Monogram Vernis, the company's signature canvas. He explains his approach saying: "Vuitton is a luxury brand – it's functional, but it's also a status accessory. I decided status would be done my way, which is to say invisibly. That means that the Vuitton logo is embossed on a messenger bag, white on white. For me that's what status is: it's absolutely not about another century or about decoration in an obvious way."[17] In doing this Jacobs gave predominance to color and texture over *griffe*. He replaced brown and beige with baby blue, pearl white, bright red, and apple green patent leather.

Jacobs' success has been so great that one critic wrote that "the word accessory is a bit of a misnomer here. For a genuine jet-set personality type – Naomi Campbell, for example – such pieces will be absolutely necessary. Even if she takes the Concorde."[18]

Karl Lagerfeld was responsible for designing the double-F *griffe* for the Italian luxury company Fendi. Hired by the Fendis in 1962 to design their furs, Lagerfeld was probably thinking of Chanel's double-C logo and Gucci's double-G when he thought of the Fendi double-F.[19] Thanks to Lagerfeld's talent as a designer and marketer, Fendi became truly fashionable for the first time.

BELOW For many status seekers, the logo is everything. Even the discreet gilt logo on Gucci's orange canvas travel bag elevates it from just another practical bag to a high-status object of desire.

Today, due to Lagerfeld's continued input (and a number of excellent advertisements), Fendi continues to be one of fashion's most prestigious names.

Fendi was established as a leather and fur workshop in 1925. Like many Italian firms producing luxury goods, it is a family-owned company. The current principals are the five Fendi sisters: Paola, Anna, Franca, Carla, and Alda, together with their husbands and children. According to Carla Fendi, when the sisters took over their parents' company after World War II there were many beautiful bags around by Gucci and Hermès, "but, perhaps because they were designed by men, they were rigid, not very convenient, like portfolios with handles. We were after softer, lighter, unlined things that suited women like us, people who work, travel a lot, need practical things."[20]

At the turn of the millennium, it sometimes seems that everyone has a Fendi Baguette. Even *The New Yorker* magazine ran a cartoon lampooning the popularity of the cult status bag. Silvia Venturini Fendi designed the Baguette. It is a small, soft handbag with a flap and a short shoulder strap. The Baguette fits just under the arm and against the breast and is carried "just like French bread" – hence the name.

Venturini Fendi has said that she was inspired by vintage bags. Certainly, the Baguette is likely to become one of those classic styles that will itself become a vintage object. The Baguette is described by Fendi as a "tiny" bag. The Fendi Croissant, its descendent, is even smaller. Many women who carry one or the other bag during the day also carry another bag for all of the things that don't fit into the Baguette or the Croissant. This does not seem to detract from their

OPPOSITE Gucci's logoed shoulder bag shot by Mario Testino attests to the power of the right brand name, and to cycles in fashion accessories. Once *the* label to be seen sporting in the 1970s, Gucci fell out of favor but bounced back in the 1990s under the direction of Tom Ford, who launched revamped versions of their classic bag designs. Ford also brought back Gucci's distinctive printed canvas – first used in the 1940s. Here it is reworked in luxurious velvet.

OPPOSITE This Dior bag is said to be inspired by the pattern of a favorite cushion on one of Mr. Dior's chairs. While its proportions are essentially modern, the bag's tinkling charm harks back to the pretty, elegant, and ultra-feminine designs of Dior in the 1950s.

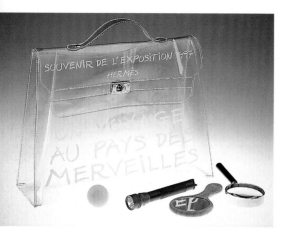

ABOVE Even made of humble materials, the Hermès bag retains its status appeal. This plastic version was made to promote an exhibition of the firm's luxury goods in Japan.

appeal. Their small size, their tactile quality, and their often ultra-feminine embellishment make them special. In fact, it almost seems as if the bag needs to be indulged, tucked carefully under one's wing, as it were.

The Baguette is a cult object in all its variations, from denim to the traditional double-F printed leather, and from crocodile to embroidered straw. There are enough variants to accommodate precious, casual, and everyday styles. The Lisio Baguette, for example, is made of silk-velvet decorated with double Fs. The fabric is produced exclusively for Fendi on old wooden looms controlled by Jacquard machines. It takes a month to prepare each loom, and only twenty centimeters of the velvet can be produced in a day. This is surely an example of precious cargo. According to Nicole Fischelis of Saks Fifth Avenue, the appeal of the Baguette derives from its "embellishment [and] luxury ... It's not just a bag with a logo. It has status appeal but offers a lot more."[21]

Fratelli Prada, a luxury leather company, was founded in Milan in 1913. Throughout the early twentieth century, Prada was known for its luggage, especially enormous steamer trunks. By the 1950s, however, the company was focusing on bags and other small leather accessories.

Miuccia Prada took over the family company in 1978. A feminist and communist in her youth, Prada was initially completely uninterested in designing bags or shoes. "I was embarrassed, since most fashion was such a nightmare for women."[22] Eventually, however, she discovered her vocation as a designer. Her first important bag was the nylon knapsack of the 1980s. As the knapsack became increasingly popular, she added a triangular metal tag, taken from the

RIGHT Fendi bags manage to project both status and street credibility. They still stand for money and exclusivity but their styling makes them hip. Amongst some fashion mavens they have become almost fetish objects. The fur Fendi photographed here by Steve Hiett for *Vogue Italia* merges the company's new-found fashionability with its traditional stock in trade.

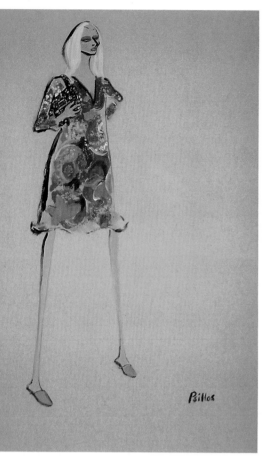

trunks her grandfather had once made. The bag with its metal triangle then became a genuine cult item. Indeed, this triangular logo is one of today's most coveted – and copied – status symbols. It has been illegally copied so often that the company warns consumers about counterfeits, and includes an authenticity card with code number in each bag.

Tod's bags are another contemporary status accessory. The D-bag, for example, has an ingenious construction, of just two pieces of leather joined down the middle. It is chic and comfortable, much like J.P. Tod's eternally popular driving shoe. The Mini Eight, a small oval bucket bag constructed in eight pieces with signature metal studs, is quickly becoming a classic evening bag.

Coach bags also have an understated luxury, but one that is distinctly American. Coach was founded in 1930 and its bags have been status symbols for American women ever since. With their smooth natural leather, rolled edges and subtle gold hardware, Coach bags are streamlined and simple with lots of "carpool cool."[23] In an attempt to position classic Coach towards the fashionable, three new lines have recently been introduced by creative director Reed Krakoff: Ergo, Tribeca, and Neo – the last named for the neoprene-like fabric used in its making.

One of the most recent status bags is the Kate Spade bag. Previously a fashion editor at *Mademoiselle*, Spade felt that the market lacked classic, simple bags in vibrant colors and interesting materials. She also thought that it was hard to find a bag that would assume each woman's individual personality, instead of making a "big statement." So in 1993 she and her fiancé launched a line of preppy, playful bags that were enthusiastically snapped up by "renegade debutantes, carpooling mothers and corporate executives."[24] Her first success was the tote bag, but she subsequently branched out into other simple styles. The fabrication is classic: black nylon, silk stripes, and tweeds, all reminiscent of Spade's American heritage – or, as she sees it, L.L. Bean meets Prada.

It has been said that: "If the eighties had a sound, it was a vertiginous swoon – as one person after another toppled over with envy at the sight of someone's killer handbag. This crashing procession of bodies – all perfectly accessorized and leveraged, prided itself on being able to spot a Chanel, and Ungaro, from a mile away. Not that this was hard."[25] Status bags are nothing if not immediately recognizable, with their "look at me logos."[26]

The status bag is even more significant today. But in contrast to the brash styles of the 1980s, status bags now provide quiet luxury and understated chic. Apparently, many women still want the prestige of a status bag but are no longer willing to risk looking like a fashion victim. Fendi and Gucci, for example, have streamlined their hardware to new levels of calligraphic and decorative effect. Marc Jacobs at Louis Vuitton has recolored baby blue the traditionally brown and black monogram canvas bag. Meanwhile, Michael Kors at Celine is creating

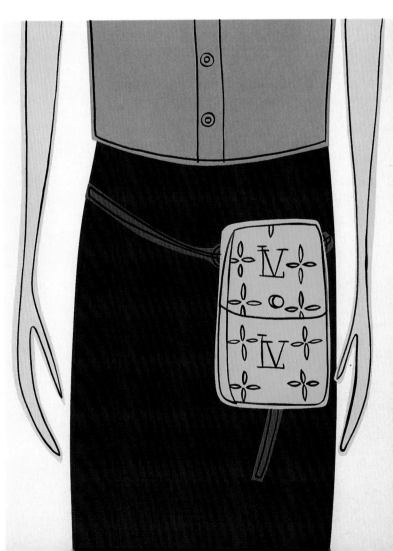

BELOW A hip Monogram Vernis bag by Marc Jacobs for Louis Vuitton drawn by Liselotte Watkins. Jacobs has managed to make the LV trademark appealing again by introducing new colors, patent leather finishes, and new shapes.

LEFT Prada is more influenced by street fashion and youth trends than most other status bag makers. By incorporating young, hip, and sporty elements into their products, Prada offers clientele of all ages the look of street-smart style together with the class, quality, and exclusivity of a high-end fashion brand.

OPPOSITE The appeal of handmade Italian leather goods has added to the success of Tod's range of bags, which are hugely popular among women who do not see themselves as label junkies but appreciate quality and craftsmanship.

RIGHT Despite the origins that it hints at, Salvatore Ferragamo's metal bag is no humble lunch pail.

BELOW Another traditional couture house that has attempted to revive its fortunes with a key accessory is Celine. Designer Michael Kors has reintroduced the French firm's "C" insignia to a range of bags, including this calfskin duffel.

OVERLEAF A stripy tote by Kate Spade, who represents a new generation of status designers.

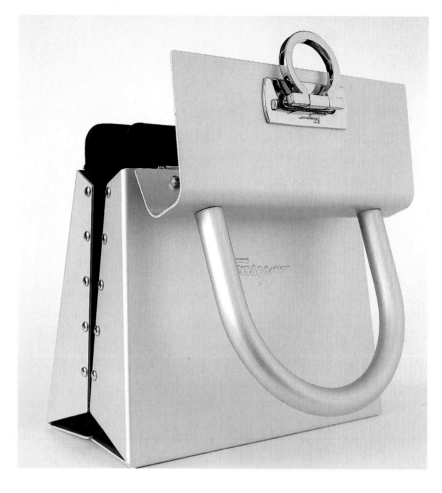

sublimely minimal collections in luxurious materials, and has reintroduced the company's archival "C" logo.

There are also economic reasons behind the contemporary craze for status accessories. Gucci, for example, makes sixty-one percent of its profits from leather goods, compared to only eleven percent of net revenue on ready-to-wear clothing.[27] Additionally, Gucci, like many other fashion companies, has recently gone public, making its profitability of concern far beyond Seventh Avenue and Bond Street. Companies are marketing bags, because they know that consumers buy status accessories more often than status clothing. The Holy Grail of contemporary luxury goods is the "Big Bag," which will be purchased by many more women than would ever buy an entire outfit. The appeal of the status accessory is summed up by Marc Jacobs, who explains: "Accessories are accessible to so many."[28] The fact that there are often waiting lists only makes them more desirable.

OPPOSITE Gucci goes glam in Mario Testino's campaign shot of the modern Gucci girl with a reworked classic from the company's past – the Jackie bag. It is perfectly in step with the times, given the millennial preoccupation with hands-free bags.

BELOW The campaign for Louis Vuitton's Monogram Vernis collection effectively portrays the bags as objects of envy, and their owners as obsessive when it comes to these particular products, appealing very clearly to the moneyed "Me" generation.

chapter four Luxury

luxury

"Your bag can be the labor of love of months by several artist-craftsmen, all lavishing on its every stage the care and professionalism and genius that goes into a couture gown."[1]

Vicki Woods

ABOVE Versace's bag has all the hallmarks of a luxury good with its glossy black alligator-skin texture and the label's distinctive, yet discreet, gilt Medusa-head logo.

OPPOSITE Nathalie Hambro's X bag is constructed by hand from articulated scales of industrial metal. Not all luxury bags are made from precious materials, but all aspire to be works of art.

Luxury signifies more than the sumptuous, opulent, and expensive. The concept also implies indulgence in pleasures beyond those necessary for a reasonable standard of life. Luxurious pleasures are of the senses, voluptuous pleasures. Indeed, the very word "luxury" once meant "lust" or "lasciviousness."[2]

Historically, the concept of luxury has been highly controversial, with many philosophies holding that luxury was pernicious to the state and a dangerous self-indulgence for the individual. A life of luxury was thought to erode moral values. By the eighteenth century, however, some economists began to suggest that luxury could play a positive role in society, as the growth of consumer desires would promote economic development and wealth, which would trickle down to benefit everyone. A compromise theory held that luxury was conducive to the development of a sophisticated and elegant way of life, but that the "abuse" of luxury could still be economically ruinous and/or conducive to immorality.[3] In today's consumer society, such debates may seem quaint.

Yet there continues to be a controversial subtext to the idea of luxury, just as there is to the idea of status symbols. Some people today believe that it is "no longer chic to be a label snob. But a lover of luxury, a sybarite, a sensualist. There isn't a human alive who doesn't get total sensual overload upon opening up a brand-new luxury leather handbag."[4] There is obviously considerable overlap between the status bag and the luxury bag, since almost all status bags are made of luxurious materials that are artfully handcrafted. But whereas the significance of the status bag centers on its name or logo, a luxury bag is usually valued "because of what it is made of, for its intrinsic value."[5]

Luxury bags are distinguished by three characteristics: 1) the precious materials from which they are made, 2) their craftsmanship, and 3) the beauty of their design, says Guiliana Camerino of Roberta di Camerino, a prestigious Venetian design company that has been in business since the 1940s.[6] Materials, craftsmanship, and beauty of design are certainly one formula for luxury. It is possible, however, to frame the issue in somewhat different terms.

"Handbags now generally fall into one of three categories: the Practical, the Status Symbol, and the Artwork," Charlotte Skene-Catling writes in her introduction to Nathalie Hambro's book *The Art of the Handbag*. She goes on to argue that Hambro has "taken the old criteria for measuring worth – beauty of form, perfection of workmanship and value of material – and enriched them with her very precise sense of irony. Nathalie Hambro produces artworks."[7]

Certainly, at some level, the luxury bag aspires to be a work of art. This is true whether it is conceived of primarily in terms of precious materials or beauty of form. Since it is virtually impossible to define terms like "art" or "beauty," let us begin with the simpler task of describing luxury materials and craftsmanship.

Luxury bags are usually made from the finest materials available. This could be high-quality leather or what the industry refers to as "exotics," such as alligator, crocodile, iguana, lizard, ostrich, python, and snakeskin. Furs such as mink and Astrakhan fall into a related category of luxury materials, as do fabrics like Fendi's Lisio velvet and di Camerino's Venetian *soparizzo* velvet, which are produced in limited quantities. The fastenings on luxury bags

ABOVE Luisa Cevese Riedizioni uses scraps of recycled fabrics to make her unique, other-wordly totes. In this case it is the hours of handcrafting involved that gives her bags their rare quality rather than expensive materials.

OPPOSITE Luxury bags display the same meticulous attention to detail as haute couture dresses. This Christian Lacroix leather bag is ornamented with a stone-encrusted antique gold resin plate.

OPPOSITE Nathalie Hambro's Inro bag is a precious work of art inspired by Japanese sash ornaments. The body of the bag is made from stainless steel gauze and embossed lead sheeting, while the twisted cord is fashioned from dulled silver threads.

ABOVE RIGHT The Hermès Kelly bag is perhaps the ultimate luxury bag. It takes approximately thirteen hours to make a Kelly and there are over 2,600 hand stitches in each one.
BELOW Valentino's red-handled tote is made from thick, black breitschwantz fur. There is no denying the symbolic association of fur with the notions of wealth and exclusivity.

are often also made of precious metals like gold and silver. Artistic handbags, however, are not necessarily made of expensive materials.

Nathalie Hambro, for example, uses a range of materials, including straw, nylon, leather, PVC, industrial metal, industrial felt, carpet tape, scaffolding sheeting, and horsehair. She uses jewelry-making techniques to create bags made of materials as disparate as electrical wire and pearls. She aims, as she puts it, to "glorify humble materials" by making them precious through meticulous craftsmanship.[8]

"I find developing new techniques rewarding," says Hambro, "and I believe in the aesthetic philosophy which says that everything could and should be made beautiful, creating a value system in which all objects large or small, expensive or cheap are of real value." An intuitive designer, she is involved with every stage of the process. Rather than sketching a design and handing it over to be produced by someone else, she taught herself to make three-dimensional paper samples of each new bag, to give herself a clearer idea of the right scale and proportions. Her inspiration can come from utilitarian objects in everyday life, the work of artists like Joseph Beuys and Robert Morris, or natural sources such as ostrich eggs. She handcrafts her bags "first and foremost for myself, to satisfy a deep sense of work ethic."[9]

It is rare that the artist herself is so intimately involved in the creation of each bag. But the making of a luxury handbag almost always involves considerable handwork by trained artisans. This is part of the appeal. Luxury bags aspire to be like couture accessories, and couture is the type of fashion that

ABOVE There is nothing quite like "the hand" of luxury materials such as ostrich. While respecting the Washington Convention, which protects endangered species, luxury goods houses use only the best materials. They also limit themselves to the prime parts of the animals, such as the chins and bellies of alligators or crocodiles, where the skin is softest.

most closely approaches art. Couture emphasizes individuality, creativity, and quality of craftsmanship.

Nathalie Hambro's bags are produced in limited editions, like works of art. Cabat I, for example, was handcrafted of bronze gauze, hand-tied with a sapphire blue leather cord, and produced in an edition of three. At Hermès, design is separated from production, but each bag is entirely made by one artisan. There is even a code for each individual bag, so that if it needs to be repaired, it can be returned to the same artisan. By contrast, a luxury bag by Tod's passes through forty hands before it is finished. Yet here, too, the emphasis is on hand craftsmanship, as opposed to mass manufacturing.

The first step in the creation of a luxury bag is usually the selection of skins or hides, and the second is the decision of how they are to be tanned or dyed.

For luxury bags, only the center of the hide is selected, and when crocodile is used, only the belly and the underside of the head and tail are selected, because these are the finest parts. Pattern pieces are then cut or punched out. At Hermès, gluing is the next step, followed by the preparation of the linings and the placement of the metal clasps and hardware between the leather and the lining. Pattern pieces are stitched together by hand or machine. (There are over 2,600 hand stitches in a Kelly bag). The final steps before delivery include cleaning, polishing, and buffing. The manufacture of a Kelly bag takes around thirteen hours. The average wait for a Birkin bag is eighteen months.

"Exclusivity. Limited distribution. Waiting lists. Drip-fed stock. These are the watchwords of modern luxury retailing," explains Woods.[10] Peter Cooper, a psychologist and commentator on consumer behavior, identifies time as an important part of the appeal of luxury goods. According to Cooper, "The relation of time to luxury goods extends beyond their fabrication to encompass their history and origins and their durability."

Bag designers Richard Lambertson and John Truex talk about the "vintage quality" of luxury exotics, explaining that they are aware of a history of glamorous women carrying bags made of luxury exotics.[12] From the 1940s through the early 1960s an exotic bag was practically *de rigueur* for fashionable women, and "matching alligator bags and shoes were an ultra-chic combination."[13] Luxury bags, especially ones made of exotic leathers, are often described as having an "heirloom" quality. The appeal of the exotic bag is confirmed by the number of ways it is imitated or simulated by embossing

ABOVE The edges on this exotic bag by Desmo recall the jagged teeth of the animal from which it was made. Designers of exotic bags often say that an individual skin can have a great deal of influence on the design of a bag. Designs are sometimes altered to better show the unique markings of skin.

OPPOSITE A Daniel Swarovski evening bag made of black diamond crystal beads and lined with a black lacquered satin pouch. Each bead is individually strung to form the intricate casing.

RIGHT This fringed pouch, also by Daniel Swarovski, is worked from shimmering crystal mesh. The swinging black silk fringe adds a Western or show-girl glamour to the already super-luxe shine of the mesh. Although precious in its dimensions, the bag's materials and craftsmanship make it essentially luxurious.

leather and synthetic materials like PVC and vinyl.

Luxury bags are often referred to as "investment pieces," both because their purchase price seems to be an investment in a particular image – and because they are supposed to increase in value. Barry Kieselstein-Cord's Trophy bag in center-cut alligator, for example, costs about $8,000. The Trophy bag has a handle flanked by two ornamental alligator heads and four alligator feet at the bottom that protect the skin at the bottom of the bag. The designer says that he saw it "as an art object; a classic for all time."[14] There is an interesting tension here, however, since – contrary to popular belief – most art does not appreciate in value over time. Of all luxury consumer items, works of art are the hardest to value, which is why art dealers tell people not to buy paintings or sculpture as an investment, but only if they really love the work.

There are other kinds of investments, however. "Investing in a good bag makes sense for a variety of reasons," writes Betty Halbeich, author of the popular advice book *Secrets of a Fashion Therapist*. "[A bag] that's large enough to carry to work every day takes a lot of wear and tear, so it needs to be high quality. It's also very visible. Like an overcoat (except that a bag is used all year round), your bag is part of the first impression people get of your style, taste, and even personality … You get a product that's made from the most luxurious materials, has a stunning design, and features first-class quality and workmanship. *That* is why it's called investment dressing."[15]

Women are not the only ones who invest in luxury handbags. "The largest group of customers for handbags and accessories as gifts are men," according

ABOVE & TOP RIGHT Grace Kelly with Roberta di Camerino's Bagonghi bag. The center panel is *soparizzo* velvet, which is manufactured by the same firm that produces velvet for the Vatican. It is made in the dark to prevent the color fading through exposure to light. No more than ten meters can be produced a month.

OPPOSITE Christian Lacroix's lavish haute couture bag is an Orientalist fantasy, made from red velvet and Afghan fabric embroidered with semi-precious stones, beads, golden thread, and golden metal leaves. It is lined in antique brocade.

LEFT Holland & Holland is famous for its hunting attire, firearms, and high-end accessories. These bags, designed by Cathy Formby, are luxuriously decorated with feathers. Formby makes the feathers, rather than the game, the prize of the hunt.

OPPOSITE The luxury associated with the 'Made in Italy' label is evident in this bag by Giorgio Armani. It is crafted from leather, which has been treated to simulate elephant hide.

to research by the National Fashion Accessories Association.[16] It seems men realize the powerful appeal of handbags to women, and know they will score points by giving a bag, rather than, say, lingerie as a present.

Certainly, a bag is an excellent gift choice, since it avoids embarrassing issues of dress size and is almost certain to be popular. Indeed, many upscale companies are also giving luxury bags to favored clients, since such a present has the enduring appeal of quality. As Wood puts it, "Luxury is unassailable, and undecorated luxury is as chic as it gets."[17]

Most luxury bags are intended to be as perfect as humanly possible. Yet the creators of artistic bags have a somewhat different perspective. As Nathalie Hambro says, "The little imperfections of a handmade bag add a certain charm that can't be found in the uniformity of a manufactured one."[18]

BELOW & BELOW RIGHT As each skin is unique, no two exotic bags are exactly alike. Spanish luxury goods house Loewe makes a bag that looks impossibly slender in profile. Jimmy Choo's tiny purse takes on the proportions of an evening bag.

OPPOSITE Barry Kieselstein-Cord's limited-edition Trophy bag is made from center-cut alligator and takes the animal association to its logical conclusion, with ornamental alligator heads on either side of the handle grasping the body of the bag with their teeth.

OPPOSITE The appeal of luxury bags is sometimes not so much that they scream expense and snobbery, but that the owner is aware of her bag's unique qualities. Giorgio Armani's tiny evening bag may look unassuming but it is woven from silk organza to give it a luxurious and tactile appeal.

ABOVE This bag, from Louis Vuitton's Epi Leather collection in Kouril black, has been dubbed the "hot water bottle bag" by the fashion press. However, the material from which it is made belies such mundane references. Epi leather is a unique material that is tanned, deep-dyed, hot embossed, re-dyed, and then glazed.

ABOVE Even the hippie look has become luxurious at the turn of the millennium. Everything about Fendi's campaign image reeks of low-key luxury, from the cashmere sweater to the Baguette bag – inspired by Indian mirror work and exquisitely crafted.

OPPOSITE Prada takes a spin on the boardwalk. Steve Hiett's photograph for *Vogue Italia* is provocative and incongruous, juxtaposing the luxurious velvety fur of Prada's breitschwantz bag against the lurid world of the funfair.

BELOW Marni's moon boots and messenger bag are made of shansi which has been dyed shocking pink. Photographed by Steve Hiett for *Vogue Italia*, they exemplify the *haute* hippie aesthetic.

OPPOSITE The concept of luxury implies indulgence in pleasures beyond the necessities of life. Tim Groen's illustration captures the pleasure of such indulgence, and of its enjoyment by an elite few – beyond the reach of the masses.

ABOVE Tod's Mini Eight is constructed from eight pieces of leather that are carefully riveted together. Like many status and luxury bags, the Mini Eight has been widely imitated. Featuring short and long straps, this luxury bag also has a practical bent.

OPPOSITE Laura B's bags resemble works of art, and, like this one of metal mesh, are individually made. The designer does not work out her creations on paper but carefully observes and touches materials, allowing them to dictate the design.

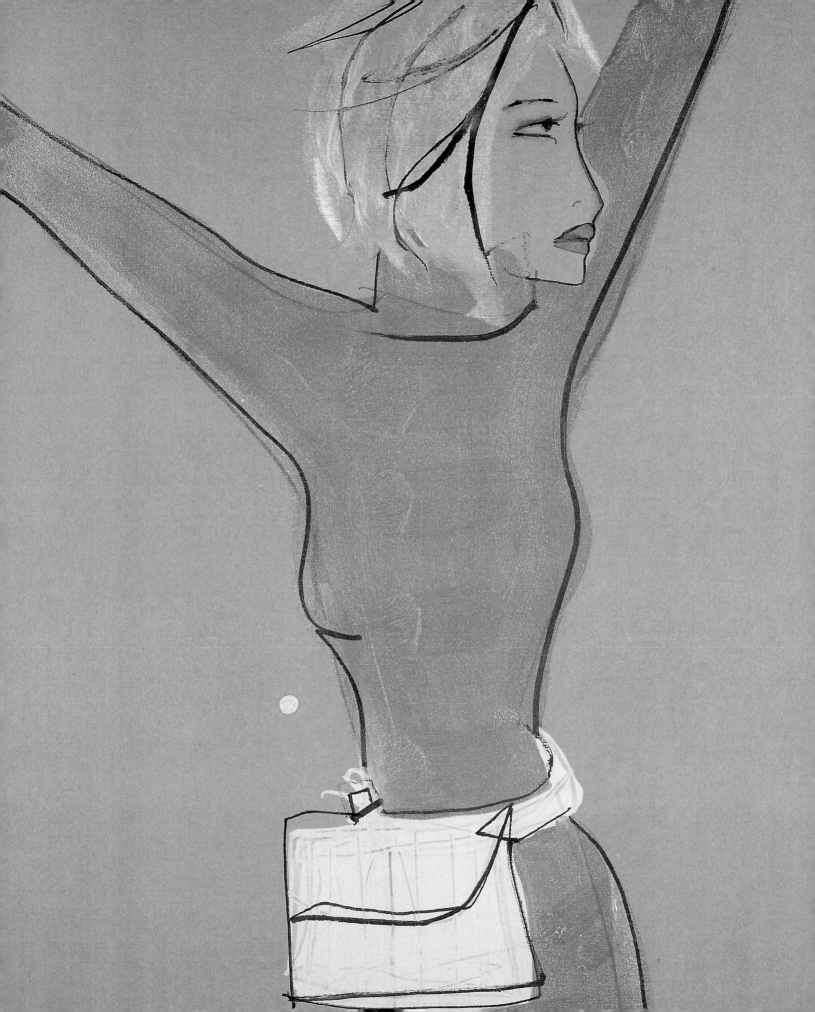

chapter five Utility

utility

"A chic woman has always clenched her bag in her fist, hung it from her shoulder or dangled it ladylike from her wrist. [Today] she simply straps a cool pack on her waist, hip or leg. Now your bag is an extension of yourself – literally."[1]   *Harper's Bazaar*

ABOVE This military-inspired bag vest, illustrated by Liselotte Watkins, is by Dolce & Gabbana and embodies the modern idea of the bag as an extension of the body.

OPPOSITE Redwall's smooth white utility bag is the ultimate in streamlined functionalism for the modern urban woman, complete with a holster pocket for a mobile phone.

Utility bags are inspired by a range of traditional, functional sources – among them military equipment, tourist gear, and sports accessories – which have been modified for modern urban life. They are sculpted to hug the body as an extension of clothing.

The first contemporary utility bag to become fashionable was the Prada backpack, which made its appearance in 1985 and quickly became an icon. It was (and continues to be) made of pocono nylon, an industrial-weight nylon used for army tents and manufactured by a parachute company. The Prada backpack was iconoclastic in terms of the company's own history of producing luxury leather goods. It also catapulted the backpack from the army, the hiking trail, and the schoolyard into the fashion arena, where it remains a staple in every fashionista's wardrobe.

The popularity of the backpack is "comparable only to the arrival of denim jeans, which also started out as functional practical items of workwear," argues fashion historian Claire Wilcox. Furthermore, she adds, backpacks are "egalitarian," because so many different kinds of people carry them.[2] It must be noted, however, that just as jeans changed when they acquired fashion status, so also have backpacks. Prada bags have been described as "cult" items, in part because they seem "subliminally sexual: all black nylon and little zippers."[3]

Diminutive backpacks made of leather and other luxury materials represent a kind of precious aesthetic more than a sporty look. Consider, for example, Marc Jacobs' mini backpack in baby blue patent leather for Louis Vuitton, which is worn high up at the shoulder blades. There are also executive-style

OPPOSITE A *haute* hip bag by Celine in white ostrich that
manages to combine the contemporary look of a messenger bag
with the glamour of luxury materials and a couture name.

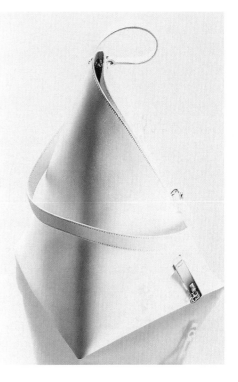

backpacks with "hard casing to protect your laptop."[4] In addition to the traditional two-strap nylon and canvas backpacks, there is the asymmetric one-strap backpack, or "J" bag, often with a pocket for a cell phone at the breast. The over-the-shoulder contour bag is said to be easier to carry than the two-strap bag, because it redistributes the weight of the bag. A *Vogue* headline shouts: "Ergomania! Slide in your G3 laptop and strap on the new body hugging bags."[5] Boblbee's rucksack is extolled because it is "designed with the twenty-first century and your spine in mind."[6] The contour bag also usually closes in front with Velcro, so the bag never has to go over the wearer's head. Because the bandoleer style strap goes across the body, it references both the messenger bag and the military style of carrying ammunition.

After the backpack became trendy, designers adapted other street styles, including various kinds of waist packs and belt bags, bum bags and fanny packs, apron bags, hip bags, vest bags, arm packs, and body pouches. Not long ago, fanny packs and bum bags were disparaged as tacky. But once designers had given the imprimatur of approval, fashionable consumers happily adopted them. Certainly, anyone interested in comfort and ease of movement had to admit that waist packs were highly functional. Indeed, as early as 1979, *The New York Times* featured an article on Sporting Gear about the "ceinture minipoches" worn by cyclists for safely carrying valuables, which featured different-sized pockets, both visible and hidden, and cost about $30.[7] Tourists, of course, have also long relied on waist bags, which provide both comfort and protection from purse snatchers.

ABOVE Salvatore Ferragamo's utility bag hooks on to the
body, becoming an extension of it. Because they are worn on
the body, utility bags can sometimes feel more like a part of one's
attire than an accessory. In fact many designers are exploring
how clothing and accessories can cross conventional dress
boundaries and serve more than one function.

RIGHT Prada's utility bags are the accessory of choice for the fashionable urban warrior, drawing on a hybrid of practical, status, and utilitarian styles. This one marries designer cachet and quality craftsmanship with hands-free convenience and military cool.

ABOVE They may be made with function in mind but many utility bags are designed to hold only a few crucial possessions, in order to retain their sleek, body hugging lines. Laid flat, this leather holster bag by Tod's is a paradigm of minimalist chic.

Because utility bags free the hands, they are often hailed as the perfect millennial accessory, which is both functional and ultra-fashionable. Yet as bag designer Laura Bortolami points out: "Although techno is the expression of the turn of the millenium, it is not revolutionary."[8] Indeed, the utility style references the very origin of the bag – a pocket tied around the waist.

The British fashion magazine *Frank* reported that utility bags are said to be "inspired by the urban environment [and] by a pre-millennial urge for self-protection and survival. But if your mind clicks more into pictures of BMX pads, pump-up blood pressure wraps and S&M, you'd be right there too."[9] According to designer Miuccia Prada: "There has to be a detail, a fabulous fabric, something unusual that puts the woman's imagination to work."[10] The military theme seems especially popular, triggering, as it does, fantasies of sex and power.

Utility bags are said to be *the* accessory of choice for today's urban warrior. Vest and holster bags, for example, are "designed to mould to your figure like armor,"and were inspired by flak jackets and bullet-proof vests.[11] These bags hold a modern artillery of cell phones and palm pilots; they leave the hands free, not so much for hand-to-hand combat, but for dialing and typing passwords. Many bags are given names that reference military terminology. Fiorucci offers an "Urban Camo Bag" and Yak Pak produces the "Wrap Holster" and the "Bomber Bag." The vogue for quasi-military bags is obviously related to the wider trend for military fashions, such as multi-pocket cargo pants.

Sports are another arena that promises to satisfy dreams of strength and glory. "Designers are increasingly looking to performance sportswear" for inspiration, reports Mark Holgate in British *Vogue*.[12] Nowhere is that inspiration more evident than in sports-inspired utility bags. Again, it is crucial to remember the backpack that Miuccia Prada made fashionable, which has sporting, as well as military, associations. Unlike purses, men as well as women carry backpacks, which have a casual appeal. In addition to rucksacks and cyclists' waist belts, designers have drawn inspiration from other kinds of sports equipment, such as fishing gear and jogging bags.

Many designers have predicted that the future of fashion is tied to fabric technology. High-tech fabrics are ideally paired, ideologically and practically, with the concept of the utility bag. Traditional materials such as canvas and leather are being superseded by industrial materials like ripstop nylon that are both strong and lightweight. Companies such as Yak Pak and Nervous Records make bags out of ballistic nylon, a fabric used to cover bulletproof vests, because it cannot easily be punctured or torn. Industrial polyester and taffeta bomber cloth are also popular techno materials. Many utility bags also have urethane coatings that ensure they are water repellant. Crypto designers

ABOVE If a nonchalant attitude is *de rigueur* for the youthful, modern woman, then the slim, hands-free waist bag, like this one by DKNY, may be her most effective accessory.

OPPOSITE In the 1980s the backpack helped to reinvent our ideas about the bag as accessory, and has since spawned a plethora of related designs. Elizabeth Powell's slim backpack draws on the cord-handled shopping bag for inspiration.

ABOVE The mass adoption of sportswear in the late-twentieth century has been key to the reinvention of the utility bag. Alongside track pants, sneakers, and baseball caps, backpacks and other sports bags have become fashion items. The logo on these Nike bags makes them especially desirable to some style tribes.

Vahap Avshar and Lexy Funk, make bags out of ink-jetted vinyl recycled from billboards, giving their bags an ecologically responsible aspect.

High-tech fastenings and hardware are also characteristic of utility bags that allow the wearer to "zip it, sling it, wrap it."[13] In contrast to the fourteen-carat gold alloy hardware used by Chanel or the signature hand-cast solid white bronze hardware and Swiss zippers used for Matt Murphy's bags, utility bags feature more industrial materials. These include buckles of plated steel, the kind of webbing used in seatbelts, 3M reflective tape, fishing zippers, nylon mesh, and lots of Velcro for easy access to multiple pockets and flaps.

But "techno" and "utility" are terms that extend beyond a reference to materials. Fashion journalists and designers alike talk about utility bags using a language that is laced with references to space and computer technology. Thus *Mademoiselle* claims that "packs and pouches prevent overload," and a vest pack offers "lots of pockets for a multitasking world."[14] Many utility bags, such as North Face's backpack, are designed to hold laptops, and therefore qualify as real power packs.

The quilted Y logo on Yak Pak's "Vexed" bag could stand for Y2K, hints Stephen Holt of Yak Pak.[15] Bags are increasingly designed for specific purposes, he adds. His company's DJ bags, for example, are designed with a round pocket for earphones, side pockets for CDs, mesh pockets for adapters and flashlights, and enough width for records. The sides can be folded down so that DJs can spin right out of their bags. Useful for real DJs, the bags have become best sellers, because they also appeal to "bedroom DJs."

A vest bag, viewed flat, or a small waist pack laid out on a table is a perfect example of minimalist chic – elegant, flat, and androgynous. But although sleek when empty, these bags often look fat and lumpy when filled with more than a credit card. This kangaroo aesthetic is not conventionally attractive, since vest bags and fanny packs conceal the sexually dimorphic curves of the female figure. As journalist James Sherwood asks, "What's the point of slipping into a delicate violet John Smedley knit sweater only to strap a thick piece of sludge-coloured canvas over it?"[16]

Utility bags are becoming more and more popular. According to *Frank* magazine, utility bags are perfect for the active young woman who "wears head spinning hardcore fashion, seeks low maintenance body perfection, pushes sex to the limit and knows that the future is here and now."[17] But what about everyone else? Observing the trend for "carry-on-your-person accessories," *Vogue* asked: "Could the handbag, so aloof and detached by comparison, soon be obsolete?"[18]

A decade earlier, the author of *Vogue Modern Style* had already suggested that "The handbag ... is no longer a priority in the world of accessory." Women might carry "another kind of bag, a satchel, say, or a briefcase, but it won't be a handbag." As of the late 1980s, "the ruck-sack ... became the bag of hip ... the bag for the urban adventurer ... The more sportif took in later months to the New York bike bag ... in tough nylon with one broad cross-over strap." To put it bluntly: "The traditional handbag is dead."[19]

OPPOSITE Ready for action, in Miu Miu's zipped, wrapped holster bag, worn over and around the body. As functional as this military-inspired bag is, it does camouflage the clothes worn underneath, making the coordination of both an important factor.
BELOW Celine's white ostrich holster bag with napa lining elevates the holster bag to luxurious heights.

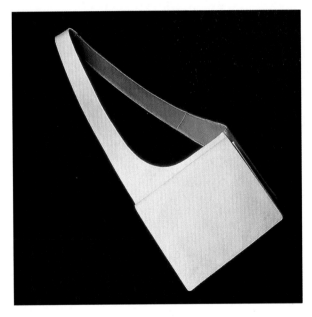

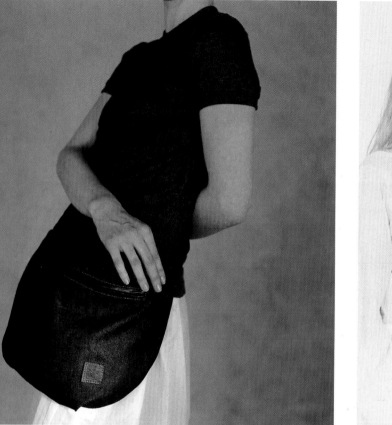

ABOVE Like denim jeans, which were originally practical articles of work wear, utility bags are egalitarian; a youth and unisex phenomenon. Amy Chan's utility bag is made of denim, while Via Spiga's versions, styled by Ernesto Esposito, are in white leather.

OPPOSITE The British design team, Vexed Generation, designs bags inspired by street culture for Yak Pak, a Brooklyn-based firm. Yak Pak's DJ bag was designed for professionals, but is also popular among "bedroom DJs". The round pocket is for headphones.

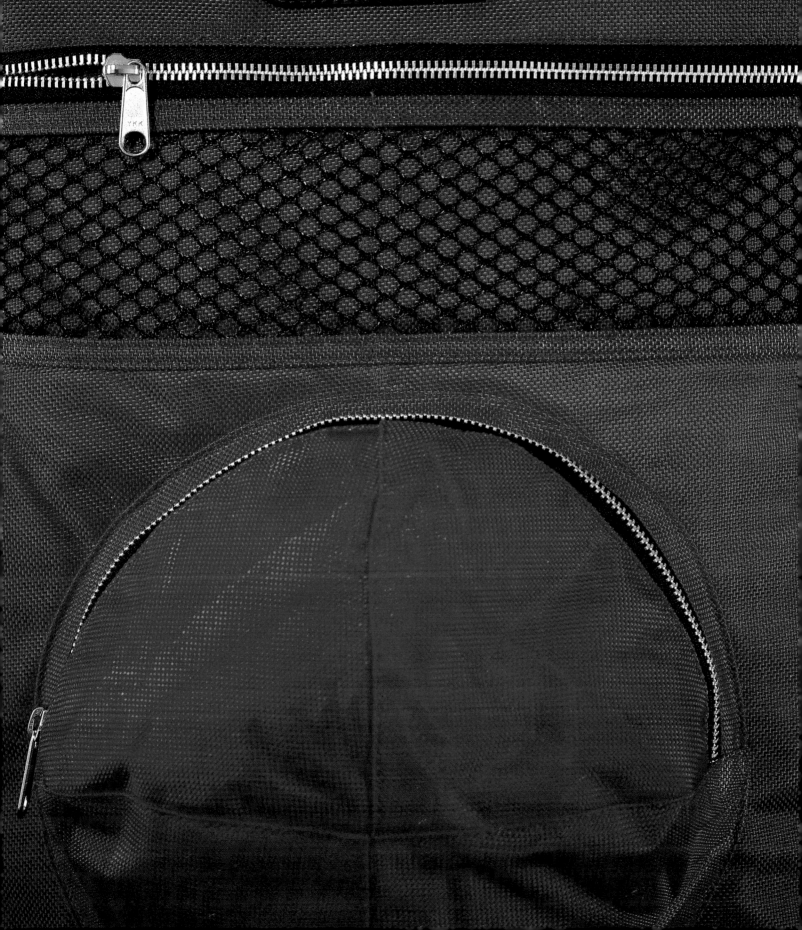

OPPOSITE Matt Murphy designed this Soleis leg holster in metallic leather. It is worn on the calf and recalls one of Mercury's wings, or ancient Greek and Roman armor.

BELOW Just like Chanel's bum pack in the 1980s, Bulgari's sophisticated backpack is more uptown than utilitarian, but is indicative of just how far the hands-free aesthetic has spread.

Despite these cries of doom, it seems highly unlikely that the handbag is obsolete, dead, or dying. Obviously, different styles of bags go in and out of fashion. We are now – and have been for a decade – very much in the middle of a long-term trend toward sporty, utilitarian fashion. This is undoubtedly an extension of the wider trend since the mid-twentieth century towards informal dress. Utility bags are not necessarily economical, however, since versions in leather, ostrich, and rubber range in price from tens to thousands of dollars. Most women will probably incorporate utility bags into a wardrobe of different kinds of bags.

Nevertheless, the rise of the utility bag is a fascinating and culturally significant phenomenon. The once shocking idea of "handbags for men" seems suddenly a possibility. As early as 1967, Gucci marketed a line in Italy of bags for men. They were then sold in America, mostly at high-end stores on both coasts. In California, for example, I. Magnin's sold Gucci satchels and Vuitton shoulder bags. An industrial designer in California admitted, though, that there were still parts of America where a man "would be eaten alive" if he dared carry a bag. The implication seemed to be that only gay men would carry bags. In fact, gay trendsetters like the designer Rudi Gernreich did carry a bag. So did author Truman Capote, who said "I don't see how people can get along without some sort of little satchel."[20] Gradually, more men began carrying bags, especially proletarian styles like messenger bags –

just as women began carrying traditionally masculine accessories, such as briefcases. Rigid gender roles were breaking down.

Utility bags are a youth and unisex phenomenon. On the streets of New York, London, and other fashion-conscious cities, some young men and women buy and wear identical bags. Young men have become freed from the bag stigma that afflicted their fathers' generation. Indeed, it is amazing to see how much stuff they carry in their utility bags. Where did they put it all before? Or did they just make do without? Meanwhile, women have been freed from the encumbrance of a conventional bag. Now the implication is that they can simply strap on, or sling over, a hands-free bag and go. One interesting question emerges from this new trend, though: Does the utility bag really improve our lifestyle, or merely make it easier to carry more around?

ABOVE Hairdressers may have begun the appropriation of the workman's tool belt for style-related purposes, but now it is has been redesigned for a wider audience. Waist-tied bag by Crypto.

RIGHT Tod's flat "Hippy" bag was inspired by 1970s-style shoulder pouches. Because utility bags free the hands, as Tod's campaign image purposefully shows, they are often referred to as the perfect millennial accessory, at once functional and fashionable.

OPPOSITE Utility bags reference the very first bags in existence – pockets tied around the waist and worn underneath clothes. Liselotte Watkins' illustration for Amica shows a total reversal. The pocket is worn, exposed, over the clothing.

OPPOSITE Many utility bags are worn bandoleer-style, like this one by Giorgio Armani. A bandoleer is an ammunition belt that is worn across the body – here implying that the wearer is equipped for survival on all terrain and ready to spring into action.

RIGHT A very old idea made ultra-modern. Laura B's metal mesh bag moulds to the body like armor, appearing to guard the body as much as provide a place for holding possessions.

OPPOSITE Bottega Veneta's fanny pack is anything but frumpy. In fact, it is the perfect accessory for the modern woman who, according to *Frank* magazine, "wears head spinning hard core fashion, seeks low maintenance body perfection, pushes sex to the limit and knows that the future is here and now."

ABOVE LEFT & RIGHT Vivienne Westwood designed this limited edition monogram canvas bum bag for Louis Vuitton in 1996. Her witty design combines a sense of the company's origins as a luggage maker and the recent obsession with functional bags.

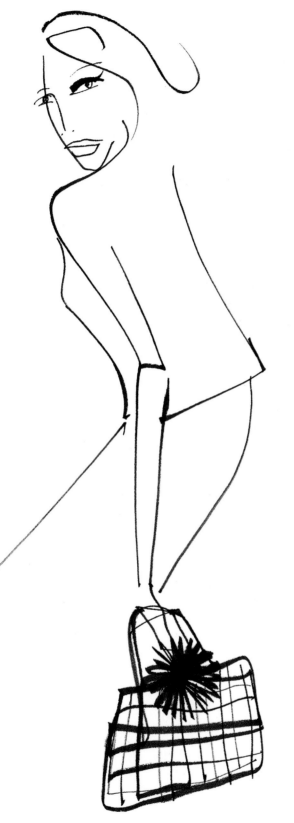

Footnotes

INTRODUCTION

1. **Claire Wilcox**, "Private Worlds in Public Places," *Satellites of Fashion*, (London: Crafts Council, October 1998), p.28.
2. **Mimi Spencer**, "Handbag Mania," Vogue (February 1998), p.242.
3. Interview with Nathalie Hambro by Laird Borrelli and Valerie Steele, 3 February 1999.
4. Tom Ford, quoted in **Spencer**, "Handbag Mania," p.245.
5. **Nathalie Hambro**, *The Art of the Handbag* (London: A Contemporary Collection, 1998), p.8.

CHAPTER 1: PRACTICAL

1. **Carrie Donovan**, "Brown Bagging It," *The New York Times Magazine* (19 April 1987), p.65.
2. "Your Wife: An Owner's Manual. Her Handbag. Its Capacity and Contents," *Esquire* (June 1990), p.154.
3. **Letty Cottin Pogrebin**, "Hers: One traditional role of women is to tote things," *The New York Times* (15 September 1983), p.C2.
4. Ibid.
5. **Mildred Graves Ryan**, *Your Clothes and Personality* (New York: D. Appleton-Century Company, 1937), p.208.
6. **Claire Wilcox**, *A Century of Bags: Icons of Style in the 20th Century* (London: Quarto, 1997), p.64.
7. **Margaret Story**, *Individuality and Clothes* (New York and London: Funk & Wagnalls Company, 1930), p.329.
8. **Christian Dior**, *Little Dictionary of Fashion* (London: Cassell & Cassell, 1954), pp.38-39.
9. **Genevieve Antoine Dariaux**, *Elegance* (Garden City, New York: Doubleday & Company, 1964), pp.112-114.
10. **Dariaux**, p.2.
11. **Saks Fifth Avenue**, *Catalogue* (Spring 1999), pp.128-9.
12. **Catherine Bennett** "Hit Her with Your Handbag, Doc" *The Guardian* (18 February 1999)
13. **Daniel Harris**, "Women's Purses: An Accessory in Crisis," excerpted in

"Plumbing the Purse," *Harper's Magazine.* (13 October 1997), p.30, from *Salmagundi* (Spring/Summer 1997).

14. Ibid.

15. Betsy Israel, "Emotional Baggage," *Working Woman* (July 1993), p.70.

16. Enid Nemy, "New Yorkers, etc." *The New York Times* (9 October 1988), p.69.

17. "Your Wife: An Owner's Manual," p.154.

18. Interview with Nathalie Hambro by Laird Borrelli and Valerie Steele, 3 February 1999.

19. Israel, p.70.

20. Sigmund Freud, *The Interpretation of Dreams, Volume V of The Complete Psychological Works of Sigmund Freud* (London: The Hogarth Press, 1953), p.384.

21. Jonathan Bell, "Q&A – Zaha Hadid," *Wallpaper** (March 1999), p.212.

22. "One in the Hand," *The Evening Standard* (23 November 1998).

CHAPTER 2: PRECIOUS

1. Christine Lennon, "Bag Ladies," *Harper's Bazaar* (November 1998), p.120.

2. Ibid.

3. Anna Sui quoted in Heidi Lender, "Getting a Grip," *Vogue* (August 1995), p.122.

4. Christian Lacroix quoted in Candy Pratts Price, "Taking the place of the lug-it-all shoulder bag: the ladylike handbag," *Vogue* (February 1991), p.360.

5. Interview with Blaine Trump by Laird Borrelli, March 1999.

6. Interview with Matt Murphy and Suzanna McDonald by Laird Borrelli, March 1999.

7. Anna Tagliacarne, "Spotlight: Artiste-artigiane," *Vogue Italia* (October 1998), p.262.

8. Interview with Nathalie Hambro by Laird Borrelli and Valerie Steele, 3 February 1999.

9. Quoted in Vanda Foster, *Bags & Purses* (London: B.T. Batsford Ltd, 1982), p.82.

10. Elaine Louie, "What's in a Handbag – Cabfare and Whimsy," *The New York Times* (8 December 1991), p.B4.

11. Quoted in Foster, p.69.

12. Interview with Lucy Sykes by Laird Borrelli, 24 April 1999.

13. Violette Noziéres press material.

14. Interview with Kazuyo Nakano by Laird Borrelli, 22 February 1999.

15. Interview with Rafé Totengco by Laird Borrelli, 18 March 1999.

16. Lender, p.120.

17. Claire Wilcox, *A Century of Bags: Icons of Style in the 20th Century,* (London: Quarto, 1997), p.64.

18. Foster, p.69.

19. "Mon truc en plus," *Paris Vogue* (December 1998), p.291.

20. "The Pleasure of Pink," *The New Yorker* (15 February 1999), p.18.

21. Elizabeth Graves, "Hi-Ho Silver," *Allure* (November 1998), p.72.

22. Interview with Saulicèia Crema by Laird Borrelli, 19 March 1999.

23. Iain R. Webb, "First Look: Embroidery," *British Elle* (February 1999), p.21.

24. Quoted in Karen Burshtein, "Stuff: A sari little purse," *The Globe and Mail* (24 September 1998), D8.

25. Angela Buttolph, "Border Crossing," *British Vogue* (December 1999), p.99.

26. Ibid.

27. Ameley Greeven, "Last Look," *Vogue* (March 1999), p.520.

28. Wilcox, p.50.

CHAPTER 3: STATUS

1. Philip Weiss, "Couture Unzipped," *Vogue* (February 1997), p.323.

2. James Ryan, "Caged Heat," *Vogue* (August 1995), p.238.

3. William Doyle auction catalogue (December 1996), p.46.

4. "Accessories Report," *Women's Wear Daily* (26 April 1999), p.10.

5. Vicki Woods, "Lust for Luxury," *Vogue* (February 1997), p.223.

6. Annemarie Iverson, "Fendi Fetish," *Harper's Bazaar* (April 1998), p.216.

7. Marina Rust, "The Big Bag," *Vogue* (August 1996), p.125.

8. Betty Halbreich with Sally Wadyka, *Secrets of a Fashion Therapist,* (New York: Cliff Street Books, 1997), p.63.

9. Lisa Armstrong, "Holding Glamour at Arm's Length," *The Times,* (2 November 1998), p.16.

10. Mimi Spencer, "Handbag Mania," *Vogue* (February 1998), p.244.

11. Janet Street-Porter, "Foodtalk," *British Vogue* (February 1999), p.173.

12. Chanel press material.

13. Shane Watson, "Give me that bag," *The Evening Standard* (16 November 1998), p.27.

14. Quoted in Richard Martin, ed. *Contemporary Fashion,* p.208.

15. Mimi Spencer, "The bags that...." *The Evening Standard* (13 March 1999).

16. Quoted in Candy Pratts Price, "Last Look," *Vogue* (January 1996), p.186.

17. Quoted in "Backstage News and Notes," *Vogue* (July 1998), p.102.

18. "The Paris Collections: Vuitton's Jet Set," *Women's Wear Daily* (9 March 1999), p.8.

19. **Richard Martin, ed.** *Contemporary Fashion*, p.157.
20. Carla Fendi, quoted in **Silvia Giaqomoni**, *The Italian Look Reflected* (Milan: Mazzotta, 1984), p.87.
21. **Iverson**, p.216.
22. Quoted in **Claire Wilcox**, *A Century of Bags: Icons of Style in the 20th Century* (London: Quarto, 1997), p.152.
23. **Ameley Greeven**, "Last Look," *Vogue* (February 1999), p.284.
24. **Chris Kelly**, "Two's Company," *Neiman Marcus: The Book* (December 1998), p.17.
25. **Cathryn Horn**, "Silent Treatment," *Vogue* (October 1995), p.146.
26. **Spencer**, "Handbag Mania," p.244.
27. **Spencer**, "The Bags that..."
28. Quoted in **Woods**, p.216.

CHAPTER 4: LUXURY

1. **Mimi Spencer**, "Handbag Mania," *Vogue* (February 1998), p.245.
2. *The Random House Dictionary of the English Language* (Second Edition Unabridged, New York: Random House, Inc., 1987).
3. **Daniel Purdy**, *The Tyranny of Elegance*, pp.17-18.
4. **Vicki Woods**, "Lust for Luxury," *Vogue* (February 1997), p.223.
5. Interview with Laura Bortolami via fax with Laird Borrelli, 16 April 1999.
6. Interview with Guiliana Camerino via fax with Laird Borrelli, 30 March 1999.
7. **Nathalie Hambro**, *The Art of the Handbag* (London: Contemporary Collection, 1999), p.8.
8. **Hambro**, p.56.
9. **Hambro**, p.47.
10. **Woods**, p.223.
11. **Peter Cooper**, "Time and Luxury," *Luxury Briefing* (September 1998), p.7.
12. Interview with Richard Lambertson and John Truex by Laird Borrelli, 24 February 1999.
13. "On the Street: Out of the Swamp, A Classic is Reborn," *The New York Times* (12 November 1989), p.65.
14. **Lindsey Van Gelder**, "Promenade Purse," *The New York Times* (7 June 1992), p.8.

15. **Betty Halbreich with Sally Wadyka**, *Secrets of a Fashion Therapist*, (New York: Cliff Street Books, 1997), p.63.
16. National Fashion Accessories Association, Inc [NFAA], "How to Sell Accessories," (NY: NFAA), p.2.
17. **Woods**, p.123.
18. **Hambro**, p. 90.

CHAPTER 5: UTILITY

1. "Body Art," *Harper's Bazaar* (March 1999), p.62.
2. **Claire Wilcox**, *A Century of Bags: Icons of Style in the 20th Century* (London: Quarto Press, 1997), p.153.
3. **Wilcox**, p.149.
4. **Annabel Tollman**, "Aerotherapy," *Wallpaper** (March 1999), p.287.
5. "Vogue's Index: 5 most wanted techno bags," *Vogue* (December 1998), p.322.
6. **Tollman**, p.287.
7. **Parton Keese**, "Sporting Gear," *The New York Times* (18 June 1979), p.C10.
8. Interview with Laura Bortolami via fax with Laird Borrelli, 16 April 1999.
9. "Free up your hands," *Frank* (January 1999), p.59.
10. **Katharine Betts**, "Miuccia Prada pulls style out of the bag for spring," *Vogue* (March 1992), p.142.
11. "Free up your hands," p.159.
12. **Mark Holgate**, "Working Wardrobe," *British Vogue* (March 1999), p.97.
13. "Pack to the Future," *Mademoiselle* (February 1999), p.101.
14. Ibid.
15. Interview with Stephen Holt and Stephen Schachtel by Laird Borrelli, 30 March 1999.
16. **James Sherwood**, "Look, no hands," *The Independent on Sunday* (7 March 1999).
17. *Frank* (January 1999), cover.
18. **Katharine Betts**, "Spring Training," *Vogue* (January 1999), p.86.
19. *Vogue Modern Style*
20. "Their New Bag," *Time* (26 September 1969), p.58.

Picture Credits

ASTRID ZUIDEMA Unit NYC, 84. BAGONGHI 146bl. BALLY, ph Steven Klein, art director Christoph Radl 16. BILL AMBERG ph Simon Upton 30c; ph Laura Challis 30r; ph Duncan Clark 72tl. BLUMARINE ph Ellen von Unwerth A/W 1995/6 collection 79. BOTTEGA VENETA ph Steven Klein 183. BULGARI ph Fabrizio Ferri 20, 176. CALVIN KLEIN cK women's Fall 1999 collection 34, 56. CARTIER 104, 112. CELINE ph Dimitri Tolstoï 36t, 111, 128bl; 173. ph Patrick Demarchelier 164. CERRUTI 1881 ph Luis Sanchez, model Carolina Muller, S/S 1999 collection 57. CHANEL 54l, 69t, 106, 107, ph Vera Atchou 109t, 109r, 110. CHLOÉ ph Liz Collins 26-27. CHRISTIAN DIOR ph J. B. Mondino 108; ph Nick Knight 62, 121. COACH 113. DANIEL SWAROVSKI ph Peter Strube, model Carole Naville (VIVA) S/S 1999 campaign 61; ph Peter Strube, model Melinda (ABSOLU) F/W 1998/9 campaign 66. DEMETRIOS PSILLOS courtesy of *Vogue*/The Condé Nast Publications Ltd. 124. DESMO ph Roxanne Lowit 10, 67, 96tr; ph Paolo Spimazzé 143. DKNY ph Mikael Jansson 169. DOLCE & GABBANA ph Steven Meisel, model Elsa Benitez 91. DOONEY & BOURKE 36bl. ETRO ph Michael Woolley 42, 76; ph Christopher Griffith 54r, 99; ph Aldo Castoldi 93tl. FENDI ph Karl Lagerfeld, model Kirsten Owen 90, 154. FRANCESCO BIASIA ph Regan Cameron for *Vogue*, models Caroline Benezet, Zofia Andrea (Marilyn) 2. FRED CORCORAN all clothes courtesy of Zambesi & Nom.D (NZ); bags Bottega Veneta, shoes Jimmy Choo 32, 33: bag Orla Keily 46-47; bags Amy Chan 51r, 98, 174; bags Daniel Swarovski 60, 92, 144-145; bags Dolce & Gabbana 70, 71t; bag James Coviello 78; bags Zoebe 80; bag Violette Noziéres 83; bag Chista 87, bag Lulu Guinness 95bl, 95tr, bags Christian Lacroix 96b, 138, 147; bag Cèia Crema 96tl; bag Mari Aoyama 97; bags Kate Spade 130-131; bag Valentino 140bl; bags Holland & Holland 149; bag Jimmy Choo 150r; bag Elizabeth Powell 171; bag Yak Pak 175; bag Crypto 177tl. GIORGIO ARMANI 148, 152, 180. GUCCI ph Toby McFarlan Pond 117; ph Mario Testino A/W 1997 campaign 118; ph Mario Testino S/S 1999 campaign 132. HERMÈS ph John Midgley 114; ph Serge Guerand 116; ph Frédéric Dumas 120, 140t; ph J von Saurma 142. HERVÉ CHAPELIER 35. HIROSHI TANABE at Kate Larkworthy 6-7. JAMIN PUECH ph Sacha Descieux & Benoît Teillet 63, 77br. JASON TANAKA BLANEY 101. JOSÉ VAN RIELE 1999/ Unit cma 21, 30l, 128tr. JUDITH LEIBER 72-73. KAREEM ILIYA 105. KENNETH COLE ph Christophe Rihet 49. KIESELSTEIN-CORD 151. LAMBERTSON TRUEX 24. LAURA B ph Gregori Civera 69br, 81, 159, 181. **LISELOTTE WATKINS** Unit NYC 125, 162, 179. **LOEWE** ph Richard Burbridge, bag designed by Narciso Rodriguez 150bl. **LOUIS VUITTON** ph Bruno Dayan, October 1998 campaign 86, 133, Monogram Vernis March 1999 campaign 38-39; ph Raymond Meier, Epi Leather May 1999 campaign 153; ph Guzman, Centennial campaign/February 1996, Louis Vuitton and Vivienne Westwood celebrate the LV Monogram 182. **MATT MURPHY** 11t; ph Elizabeth Young, model Kristine (DNA), Spring 1999 collection 177r. **MAURICE SCHELTENS** Unit NYC 45. **MAX MARA** ph Steven Meisel, model Carolyn Murphy 15. **MISSONI** ph Mario Testino 29; ph Mario Testino, models Angela Lindwall, Tasha Tilberg, Vivien Solari 50, 100. **MIU MIU** 172. **MULBERRY** ph Don Freeman, A/W campaign 1998/99 28. **NANNINI** 14, 18t. **NATHALIE HAMBRO** ph Jonathan Lovekin 64, 137, 141. **NEXT DIRECTORY** S/S 1999 collection 25r. **NIKE** 170tl, 170cl. **PATRICK COX** S/S 1997 campaign 55. **PERRY ELLIS** 19. **PHILIP TREACY** S/S 1999 collection 68, 71br. **PIET PARIS** Unit NYC 9. **POLLINI** ph Livio Mancinelli 187. **PRADA** 43, 126-127, 166-167. **RAFÉ TOTENGCO** ph Mei Tao/Frame 94. **REDWALL** ph Malena Mazza, graphic agency, Christoph Radl, producer, Camilla Invernizzi, coordination Redwall advertising office 44l; ph Malena Mazza, art director Christoph Radl 163. **LUISA CEVESE RIEDIZIONI** 139. **ROBERTA DI CAMERINO** ph Manfredi Bellati (1968) bags "Chopin" & "Listz" 85; *L'Europeo* magazine cover 146l; bagonghi bags 146r. **RODO** ph Paolo Spimazzé 17; ph Oriani & Origone 18l, 74. **RUDY FACCIN VON STEIDL** © Rudy Faccin von Steidl 115. **SALVATORE FERRAGAMO** 25t, 165. **SERGIO ROSSI** ph Miles Aldridge 48, 52. **SONIA RYKIEL** ph Mario Testino 41, 75, 93br. **SOTHEBY'S** Christian Lacroix handpainted evening bag Spring 1999 collection, donated by Christian Lacroix for CRIA "To have and to hold" handbag auction 65. **STEFANO PAOLILLO** bag Orion, model Laura Pedone 26l. **STEVE HIETT** 22-23, 122-123, 155, 156. **TANNER KROLLE** ph Hans Gissinger 37, 88, 89. **TANYA LING** courtesy Bipasha Ghosh/William Ling Fine Art 4, 12-13, 58-59, 102-103, 134-135, 160-161, 184. **TIM GROEN** Unit NYC 157. **TOD'S** 31; ph Giovanni Gastel, model Yasmin le Bon, 129, 158, 168, 178. **VERSACE** 11b, 136l. **VIA SPIGA** ph Livio Mancinelli 174. **VIOLETTE NOZIÉRES** ph Tasco Puplick 192. **WALTER STEIGER** 82. **ZANNA** stylist Lucinda Alford 53l, 53r.

acknowledgments

Both the publisher and authors would like to thank the following for their generous assistance:

AMEDEO ANGIOLILLO, AMY CHAN (*Alan Chan, Owen Davidson*), ANTONELLA MAZZA, ART & COMMERCE (*Andrew Thomas*), ART PARTNER (*Candice Marks*), ASTRID ZUIDEMA, BALLY (*Louise Rowles*), BARRY KIESELSTEIN-CORD (*Pam Eldridge, C.C. Twing*), BELLA FREUD (*Cozette McCreery*), BILL AMBERG (*Amanda Lanchberry*), BLAINE TRUMP, BLUMARINE (*Lara Mazza*), BOTTEGA VENETA (*Nadia Rebbecato*), BRIDGET AUSTIN, BULGARI (*Anna Zalewski/Aurelia*), CARTIER (*Lucianne Wainwright*), CAROLYN KRAEMER, CÉIA CREMA, CELINE (*Blandine Viry*), CERRUTI 1881 (*Claire Berthoud, Jacques Babando*), CHANEL (*Marika Genty*), CHISTA (*Daphne Dor, Tom Lowery*), CHLOE (*Victoria Hennessy*), CHRISTIAN DIOR (*Christal de Rougenont*), CHRISTIAN LACROIX (*Nathalie Jalowezak*), CHRISTIANE CELLE, CHRISTOPH RADL, CLM (*Felix de N'Yeurt*), CK CALVIN KLEIN (*Jennifer Yu*), COACH (*Blish Mize*), CRYPTO (*Lexy Funk & Vahap Avshar*), DANIEL SWAROVSKI (*Mathilde Janson*), DEMETRIOS PSILLOS, DESMO (*Annastella Terranova*), DKNY (*Jana Gold*), DOLCE & GABBANA (*Anja Kohne*), DON FREEMAN, DOONEY & BOURKE (*Phyllis Dooney*), ELIZABETH POWELL, EMMA HOPE (*Pauline Higgins*), ETRO (*Rossella Colombo*), FENDI (*Patrizia Nave*), FRANCESCO BIASIA (*Mitch Handler*), FRED CORCORAN, GIORGIO ARMANI (*Juliet Longcroft*), GUCCI (*Kat Roberts*), HANS GISSINGER, HERMÈS (*Lucy Nicholls*), HERVÉ CHAPELIER, HIROSHI TANABE, HOLLAND & HOLLAND, JAMIN PEUCH (*Emilie Haron/Univers Presse*), JAMES COVIELLO (*Lisa Kempf*), JASON TANAKA BLANEY, JIMMY CHOO (*Hannah Colman*), JOHN ERIC, JOHN.J GAVIGAN, JOHN S. MAJOR, JOHNATHON GREGSON, JOSÉ VAN RIELE, JUDITH LEIBER (*Catherine Carmichael*), JULIAN MEIJER (*Philippe Brutus*), KAREEM ILIYA, KATE LARKWORTHY, KATE SPADE (*Justine Swerdloff*), KENNETH COLE, KIMBERLY SCHRETER, LAMBERTSON TRUEX (*Richard Lambertson & John Truex, Amanda*), LAURA B (*Laura Bortolami & Gregori Civera*), LISELOTTE WATKINS, LIZ CLAIBORNE (*Lucille Dearheart, Karen Tillson*), LOEWE (*Maya Maini*), LOUIS VUITTON (*Marie-José Lauer, EURO RSCG*), LUCY SYKES, LUISA CEVESE RIEDIZIONI, LULU GUINNESS (*Charlotte MacFarlane*), MARI AOYAMA, MARIO TESTINO, MATT MURPHY, MAURICE SCHELTENS, MAURITZA SCOTCH, MAX MARA (*Silvia Fornasier, Holly Vogel, Giorgio Guidotti*), MICHELA MORO, MISSONI (*Susanna Colleoni*), MIU MIU (*Verde Visconti*), MONIQUE JARVIS FOR ZAMBESI + NOM.D (NEW ZEALAND), MONTANA LEE, MULBERRY, NANNINI, NATHALIE HAMBRO, NATHALIE HATGIS, NEXT, NIKE (*Mark Rhodes*), ORLA KEILY, PATRICK COX (*Andy Lipscombe*), PATRICK MACDONALD, PERRY ELLIS, PHILIP TREACY, PIET PARIS, POLLINI (*Leila Palermo*), PRADA (*Verde Visconti*), RAFÉ TOTENGCO (*David St. Gelais*), REDWALL (*Marilli Alessandretti*), REGAN CAMERON, ROBERTA DI CAMERINO (*Guiliana Camerino & Erica Pellati*), RODO, RUDY FACCIN VON STEIDL, RUPERT TENISON, SALVATORE FERRAGAMO, SERGIO ROSSI (*Sara Negri*), SONIA RYKIEL (*Candice Dupon*), STEFANO PAOLILLO, STEVE HIETT, STEVEN MEISEL, SUZI FUNAHARA, TANNER KROLLE (*Jamie Kenny/Leagus Delaney*), TANYA LING, TARA FERRI, TASCO PUPLICK, TASSIO/ITALY (*Kenneth Wittman*), TIM GROEN, UNIT NYC (*Jasper Bode*), TOD'S (*Paola Magis*), VALENTINO (*Carlos Souza*), VERSACE (*Petra Walton/Aurelia PR*), VIA SPIGA (*Ernesto Esposito, Sharon Williams*), WALTER STEIGER (*Nancy Mizrahi*), YAK PAK (*Stephen Holt & Stephen Schachiel*), YANNICK MORISOT, ZOEBE (*Karin Zoebelein*).